Earthly Use

Earthly Use

New and Selected Poems

Kate Bernadette Benedict

Umbrella Editions
New York City

Copyright © 2015 by Kate Bernadette Benedict
All rights reserved.

ISBN 978-0-692-39313-0

Cover and interior image: "Smoke" by Leung Cho Pan
Cover and interior design by the author

For My Niece and Nephews

JaneA
Michael
Damon

Contents

The Bunting
The Bunting / 3
A Fine Form of a Man / 4
Warts and All / 5
Feet / 7
Helen Agonistes / 8
Night Crawlers / 9
Eels / 11
Wild Women of Borneo / 12
Meta-physical / 13
Adipose Ode / 14
Holding Up / 15
A Woman, Childless by Choice / 16
Resolution / 17
Sheela-na-gig / 19
Continuum / 20

Dark Nights
Knees / 23
Dry / 24
Dread / 25
Contempt / 26
A Strange Mazy Life / 27
Continuous Play / 31
The Unforgiving / 32
The Apartment / 33
The Holy Name / 34
The Essay / 35
The Intruder / 37
Night Terrors Happen in the Rift of Time / 38
Cinema Verité / 39
Earthly Use / 40
How I Responded to the Invitation / 41

The Polis of Sorrow
The Polis of Sorrow / 45
The Washer at the Ford / 46
The Stinky Lady / 47
The Two / 49
Early Lessons: Barbarity / 50
When Girls Fight / 51
Once In, Never Out / 52
Starstruck / 53
The Moment / 54
Rodin: The Gates of Hell / 55
We Are Refugees / 56
Shrapnel / 57
The Birth of the Blues / 58
The Cause / 59
We Had Fun / 61

There. Within.
Here From Away / 65
There / 66
Within / 67
When the Elephants Took Me for their Pet / 68
Amniotic Man / 69
American Highways / 70
A Journalism of the Soul / 71
Gulf Coast Gothic / 73
In This Church / 74
In the Devil's Monastery / 75
The Exorcist of Alcatraz / 76
Maximum Security / 77
The Carrion Gardens /79
On the Plethora of Visions / 80
The Architect / 81

The Common Room

Romeo's Soliloquy / *85*
Early Lessons: The Quest / *86*
Recognition / *87*
According to Kitty / *88*
The Common Room / *89*
The Sureties / *91*
Neighborly Elegy / *92*
Island Trail / *93*
Night of the Comedians / *94*
The Suicide Memorial / *95*
Autumn Weekend in Vermont / *97*
The New England Poets / *98*
Expedition in Mid-life / *99*
The Burning Cloud / *101*
When I Am Old / *102*

A Man and a Woman

The Keepers / *105*
Preparation for the Dance / *106*
In the Key of Snow / *107*
Glimpses of the Body in a Modest Household / *109*
Florida Love Bugs / *111*
Florida Palm Trees / *113*
Sick / *114*
Tantalizing Sestina *115*
Almost / *117*
That Place / *118*
Into His Hand / *119*
Off the Road / *120*
A Man and A Woman Descending A Stair / *121*
Supplication / *123*
Hope / *124*

In Company

Words for a Temp / *127*
Green Man / *128*
Universe Management / *129*
Torpid Transit / *131*
Invitation to a Baby Shower in the Corporate Law
    Library / *132*
Waiting for Elevation / *133*
Travailelle / *134*
After Long Days Visiting the Nursing Home,
    I Return to the Office / *135*
The Triumph of Eros / *136*
High Floor Ballad / *137*
A Roadblock in the Negotiations/ *138*
Love and Work / *139*
After / *140*
In Company / *141*
The Transformation / *142*

Lovechildren

Lovechildren / *145*
The Forgotten Prophets / *146*
What Goes Around / *147*
The Spell Weaver / *148*
The Ritual / *151*
Money: A Valediction / *152*
Salvific Ode / *153*
Sociable Ode / *154*
Rienelle / *155*
Light on Water / *156*
The Widest River / *157*
Atlantic City Idyll / *159*
The Awkward Age / *160*
The Sociability of Nations / *161*
The Frozen Sea Within / *163*

Nothing. Not Nothing.
What Pervades / *167*
She / *168*
Self as a Refuge / *169*
Dust and Sin / *170*
The Incompetent Mystic / *171*
The Elderly Atheist / *173*
Sister Rigor Mortis / *175*
On the Mercy of the Gods / *177*
A Score for Reverend Jack / *179*
Charitable Deductions / *180*
The Very Rich Hours / *181*
Salutation to the Sun / *182*
Indra's Net / *183*
Contemplative Observances / *184*
Come to the Dance / *185*

A Few Notes / *189*

Acknowledgments / *191*

Author's Preface

"Let me extol the uses of denial/imperiled in this age of trite sincerity!" This wry exclamation begins one of the poems in this collection. Now let me extol something else: a formerly acceptable but now imperiled custom: self-publishing in an age of credentials and careerism. Many poets—indeed, many fine poets—follow the rule book: get an advanced degree, often an MFA; network one's way into journals; win a book contest or two; muster up some grants. And the number one rule in the rule book: never publish your *own* book. There's no prestige in it.

I confess I wouldn't mind a little prestige wafting in my direction, but it seems I possess a contrarian 'tude that makes the scenario unlikely. Academia is not my thing. Currying favor? Not so much. For many years, I did enter book contests, writing out checks and mailing off manuscripts, but it was a fool's quest. Eventually, I found a publisher for two collections but decided to buy back my rights. Retaining one's rights is a significant advantage of self-publishing. How I wince, remembering that I relinquished all rights, everywhere, for the life of the contract, and received in return nothing more than a print-on-demand book and an obligation to buy it in quantity. I even had to supply a printer-ready .pdf file, blurbs, and a cover image. That was the deal.

That was the deal and it was not a vanity press. Unless a poet is snapped up by a major publishing house or university press, she or he is likely to encounter the same situation, or something similar. Friends of mine—masterful, spirited poets—accept the indignities more cheerfully than I do. The arrival of that fragrant box of books makes up for a lot.

If you are reading these words, then I too have in my possession a fragrant box of books, and they cost far less than those purchased with my old, contractual 40% author's discount. A fatter wallet is another perk enjoyed by those who are "doing it for ourselves." But control is the biggest advantage of self-publishing, at least for me. Control over content, control over length, the satisfaction of not only writing the book but designing it, inside and out. Having worked as a book editor for major publishers, and having published a trifecta of online poetry journals, I felt I was up to the task. Still, it was a steep and dizzying "learning curve" — I'd had no experience in book design or specifications — but how invigorating to finally prevail! The satisfaction is prestige enough, but then again, I am one to praise the uses of denial.

A few words, now, about *Earthly Use*. The common practice is to separate "new" uncollected poems from those previously collected, but I thought that arranging poems into thematic sections would be more interesting, and I hope the reader finds it so. The poems were written over a span of four decades, and after such a span, one's obsessions become clearer, one's convictions firmer. I'm in the book.

Formal acknowledgments begin on page 191. Less formally, I'd like to thank my abiding husband John, as always. Thanks, too, to my gifted poetry friends from the Carmine Street Metrics gang; you coaxed me out of a hidey hole and you continue to inspire me.

The Bunting

THE BUNTING

Who would escape the flesh,
lodged as we are within it?
Without, no eye turns inward, no palm upward.
No hum or hymn or whisper;
no hosanna, no hush.

With age, my mother's eyes grew clouded.
Her spine warped.
Veins resembled earthworms after rain,
bloated and abounding.
She moaned: her joints scraped.
She could barely lift a spoon
and struggled with her straw.
"Grandma isn't ready to leave her body yet,"
my niece remarked.
Tasting blood, I chewed my lip and nodded.

Body, O flesh,
keep me tucked a little longer in your bunting,
however frayed the cloth.

A Fine Form of a Man

. . . was what my father called himself.
Fine form: the bald, soft pectorals.
Fine form: the flabby, rolling girth.

Mention one of his manifold abnormalities—
the crooked nose wart,
the swollen ankles, streaked and raw,
the toenail humped and earthy as a truffle—
and he'd smile, his green eyes twinkling.
You'd paid him homage.
You'd noticed a fine particular
of his excellent form!

A rare endowment, is it not,
to bear your flawed flesh royally,
blubber your vesture,
fungus your rare black pearl?

Even pain conveyed a certain stateliness
the way my father braved it,
without complaint or folderol.

One day he sawed and sanded, shirtless in the sun,
blisterings emblazoning his back.
I touched the largest one; he didn't flinch.
I offered ointment; he scoffed!

He scoffed, he burned,
and still he held the monstrance of his body high
that all might venerate.
And thus we gathered round him to partake.

Warts and All

    As it happens, they run in the family—
those skin slubs, those strange barnacles
      that make rough prow of chin, jowl, neck.
          Tentacles

    of pink jelly, they curl bewitching
fingers out of heirloom photographs, or push
      up like delicate mushrooms in moist,
          itching

    places. My father's poked from the side
of his nose, in that crook beside the nostril's
      oval flare. Over the course of years, that
          hill

    of a wart sprouted a wart of its own
and around the base, plum capillaries leaked
      forked tributaries to the fertile whiskered
          cheek.

    My own cheek burned when a puckish cousin
climbed in his lap, pressed her thumb to
      the growth and loudly asked "What's that?"
          "Brat!"

    I shrieked, ripping her off him. Now
as I voice this late encomium, it's her innocent
      interest I root for. Kids knew somehow
          his

    wart defined him: Uncle Eddie
with the deep voice and the populous nose! Time
      and again, mother counseled
          him

    to accept the surgeon's
beautifying knife, but she loved its unloveliness
      anyway, I think, for its home-sweet-
          homeliness,

  its guilelessness, for comic relief
whenever he raved or harped. Even in the coffin,
  under pancake, it made us grin,
    poking up

  wonkily, doing a little hula in
in our welling eyes. We knew how much
  we'd loved him then—
    warts

and all, as the saying goes. Years later
as I approach the era of age spots and other
  such atrocities, a clone-like
    brother

  of that wart presumes to mess
this otherwise immaculate
  complexion! "Bad
    cess

  to it," my Irish grandma would have said—
but fingering the odd, wobbly protuberance
  I laugh, and welcome the undignified
    inheritance.

Feet

Size 12-and-a-half, my nephew boasts,
stretching his frisky toes
before this roomful of small-footed women.
He's sprawled on the recliner,
his feet held high
in the stifling apartment air.
Aunt, mother, grandmother—
all day we have laced up our emotions
like the sneakers Michael tore off so eagerly;
all day our eyes have worn a blank, white-sock look.
And now these honest feet intrude on our lies.
We note the frank arch, the forthright heel,
the endearing lack of stink or callous,
while dank under hot leather
our orange corns grow horned,
our ruddy bunions rub and pulse.
Let's see *your* feet, Aunt Kate, he teases,
but I sit on them instead
and keep what's best kept hidden, hidden.

HELEN AGONISTES

The hair dye kit is rent, the potions blended,
the applicator bottle top is snipped.
Around Aunt Helen's neck a towel is draped,
an ancient cloth of stained and ragged weave.
My mother combs away the stubborn snarls
as Helen utters syllables of woe
and then along the hairline smears a gel
to minimize the mixture's stain and sting.
Mother scores the hair in even parts,
methodical as Circe at her spinning,
serene in deed as any Grace or Muse.
And thus in latex gloves she squirts and daubs,
she saturates each hoary root and strand.
Such noxious fumes suffuse the kitchen air!
Helen squeezes eyes against the vapors
and whimpers a complaint: the goop is cold.

At last the head is drenched, the bottle empty.
Painted Helen sighs and plays canasta
until the timer sounds its saving bell.
A long shampoo is next, and many rinses,
till curler-crowned she dons the bonnet dryer.
Part hornet now, part woman, and part snake,
a changed Aunt Helen sits under that dryer
which emanates abysmal hiss and buzz.
Tobacco vapor spirals from her nose.
When her hair is dry and out of curlers,
all woman once again and sleekly styled,
she stands before my mother's Grecian mirror
and poses for my flabbergasted father.
Like another Helen, young and new,
she strides into the street with swaying hips
to launch a widow's Sunday night alone,
to launch a thousand nights alone, not ships.

Night Crawlers

Cool as skin after a swim,
that rock,
heavy as a secret.

We peeled it back
from the yard's muscle.

Ted's flashlight
showed three slugs
hugging the bottom.

Jon pried one off
and Ted petted it.

Its little twin head-stalks
stood up and reached!

Under us, the lawn
seemed jumpy. Over us,
the streetlamp's halo buzzed.

Nobody said much.

Then, tender as anything,
Jon put the slug down,
the rock back.

Later we swiped fireflies
from the sticky air—
cupped them, smelled them,
stroked them, let them go.

Jon and Ted
kept to themselves
for the rest of the summer.

Linda and Laura and I
did the usual stuff.

But nothing I buttoned Barbie into
fit right
and play-school seemed stupid.

My mother kept accusing me
of sulking.

I wasn't sulking!

I was living it again—
that humming, humid night

when the boys
let me crouch with them
in the damp August grass,

inspecting night crawlers.

Eels

. . . in the pail, looped like bowels in their salt
broth, a spectacle of rolling shudders.
Close odors! One slimy writher butters
its brine with a slick spit. I find no fault

with it, though other kids flinch and go *eeew eeew*
when I tell them I have eels for dinner. Daddy hooks
and hauls them out of the choppy Sound. Such looks
he gives me! They dangle in his hand and slurp-spew.

Home, at the sink, he denudes them of their skin.
A few slits, a long yank: it's a cinch to strip off.
Then mother chops them and hums, dredging the soft
lumps in a dune of cracker meal. What a din

as she slides them into the frying pan! The cat
trots in, hoisting a tail to the feast in that hot fat.

Wild Women of Borneo

. . . was what a red-faced, stamping nun
called the eighth grade girls
who bleached and teased their hair
into moonlit jungles,
whose ripe mango breasts
pressed against their uniform jumpers,
whose pierced ears glittered
with dangles, studs, and hoops.
Wild Women of Borneo:
strobe-lit at the Christmas mixer,
rocking and rolling in barefoot ecstasy.
Wild Women of Borneo:
snapping their fingers high.
Hidden behind my books,
I watched them smoking in the alleys,
their private rite.
Singing to the Virgin Mother,
I saw them primp at holy mass,
their minds on no immaculate conceptions.
They favored white lipstick, black slips,
a perfume called Tabu—
I tell you, I studied those girls
the way I studied my catechism,
reading them for questions,
memorizing their answers
and never quite solving
their glorious mysteries.
O Wild Women of Borneo,
that red-faced, stamping nun who gave me
A's and praises never guessed
with what transfixion my heart attended you
or with what unrest.

META-PHYSICAL

A shaman in a white garment
peers with his instrument into my ears,
gauging their sensitivity to the concordances.

He shines a light into my eyes,
to read what testament may be written there.

He inspects my skin for malignant signs.

He palpates, probing for deviations;
he inserts a prognostic hand.

An acolyte draws blood into small glass ampoules,
placing them in a tabernacle marked with a red cross.
I wear her arm band.
Mildest of penance, that viselike embrace.

I am sent off for a scansion of the bone,
for I am an ossuary and worthy of rapt regard.

An advent follows.
At last I receive the *imprimatur*.
I am pronounced fit.

Holy day!
I observe it with fresh juice in a goblet
and a supper of bread and olives.
I meditate, I assume the poses:
thunderbolt, hero, tree.

Adipose Ode

O greediest of cells, hoarder of calories,
simian gourmand stuffing your cheeks even as we sleep,
it's time we honored you for a job well done!
Thanks to you we sit comfortably in pew and on barstool,
our laps make soft perch for sad child and weary head.
In this age of shove and jolt, you cushion and buffer.
But for you our sharp bones jangle, jut, and bruise.
Lush flesh, I celebrate your excess, your allure.
What lean limb, what gaunt hip, could possibly compare?
It is the fashion to be angular as a hanger, a skinny horse
for one's clothes, it is stylish to wear one's muscles like armor.
But I say: soften your edges, let your fat jackself
out of that narrow box, feed your body well
and maybe your soul will increase along with it
and the world be charged with an adipose grandeur,
a contentedness, a magnanimity, a benevolent queen-size swell.

HOLDING UP

So many things need buttressing—
books, walls,
my elderly neighbor inching down the hallway
with his aluminum walker,
braced also by his burly roommate.
I can't keep my eye from the peephole.

So many things need shoring up—
grape vines, wisteria,
the floppy heads of infants
whose life depends
on the stanchion of the large people's palms.
A colleague broke her neck
on the slopes of Reach Mountain.
Ice, flight, fall—
from inside the metal scaffold they'd pinned her in,
she'd retell the story.

I have fractured no vertebra myself
but years ago my sustaining spirit broke
and never fully mended.
Luckily, even a broken thing has utility
if you glue it and re-glue it and keep it around.
Devotedness is a buttress too.
Daily, through my peephole, I witness it in action
as a buddy holds up a buddy,
guiding him down the hallway,
ushering him home.
The old man weeps, or warps his mouth;
the younger man bears it.
I prop my heavy head
on my heavy door
and watch.

A Woman, Childless by Choice

"The tree of life and the tree of life
unloosing their moons, month after month, to no purpose."

— *Sylvia Plath*

What moment is this?
I have passed into a calm finality.
I was a woman who might have children,
and now a woman who never will.
A metamorphosis—
one pictures a turbulence—
but all I feel is the empty womb, emptying.
Can anyone be less encumbered?
The lightness of my load astounds me.

And still
"the tree of life and the tree of life"
fulfill their purpose.
Readiness
comes and comes,
readiness
keeps and fills—
there is no emptiness.
I walk in plenitude, as women do.

RESOLUTION

Toy horns shrieking, real ones moaning:
as one year keened into the next
and I drank to the old one's let-down,
the new one's promise,
and kissed—indiscriminate!—any mouth
that leered in front of my mouth in the crowd
and met the random crush of strangers' thighs . . .

then and there, I resolved to become more spiritual.
Prayer would start each day and end each night.
The veiled sisters who once drilled me in piety?
Their modesty would be my model, their humility my pride.
From a trunk in the loft I would raise the Ignatian Way,
swap Caritas for Eros, church for brunch,
and when the new year next wailed into morning
you would dub me Mahatma: holy, great-souled.

I resolved to become more spiritual
but O Lord, I have become more carnal,
in thought lustful, in deed wanton,
dragging through my days in a haze of sexual burning,
stoking the coals by night and day and night.
I would wrap my legs around anything,
man or ape, such is the depth of my want. I want!
And what I want I will have by any means.

The sisters taught: the body is a temple
of the holy spirit, a shrine, but keep it shrouded.
I unshroud, I show myself, my every secret part,
crying look, look on me,
look, husband, look, mirror,
look, angel, on what never will be your home!
John Donne, praying to be chaste,
in erotic frenzy called on God to ravish him.
Ravishment is the issue.
Sensation is the issue.
That which begins
and builds
and builds

and bursts you open
until the strife of body and soul
reach, for a rhapsodic moment, resolution.

I resolved to become more spiritual.
Hear me, O Lord: I have.

Sheela-na-gig

Disquieting, this spectacle of flesh:
hunching hag with massive nether lips.
Her two hands spread them open in a gaping nether leer.
She puts the fear
of God in all who look. All look.

She's said to be a sign of mortal sin,
a warning to the penitent: keep chaste
or fall into a mouth like Sheela's mouth, insatiable.
Monk, layman,
beware the awful chasm of desire.

Or is she more a totem or a charm
whose magic may avert the evil eye?—
for such depictions cast away the devils of the night,
it's said,
who stalk the undefended souls of travelers.

Appalling mouth and mouth beneficent,
portal of death and portal too of life,
you impart a vital power even as you horrify.
That's why
witches and midwives keep a Sheela near.

If Sheela's mouth could speak! But she is mute,
her open maw of stone, stone still.
Sculpture strange and commonplace, guileless, grotesque,
lewd, squat,
most holy, most unholy, unstatuesque.

Continuum

Birth,
milk,
the supple muscle meat of us,
that we pounce and chatter,
our brutal eye—
yes, we are animal.
Seized by fierce exhaustion,
daily we sleep;
daily we wake
with an indolent leonine yawn.

Breath,
thirst,
the bifurcated root of us,
that we are tied to earth
but turn toward light—
yes, we are vegetable.
In green calm,
daily we grow;
daily we wilt.
Shall we embrace the wilting?

Tooth,
bone,
the lacerated facets of us,
that we are molten, many-layered,
massive, pebble-light—
yes, we are mineral.
Inert, of earth,
daily we are mined,
daily the waves wash over us.
We ring.

Dark Nights

Knees

And so I am brought to them again.
In this posture, on this gravel floor,
all my bones are numbered.

The pieties of childhood, the bedtime prayers,
have nothing to do with this ignoble humbling.

A sorrowful mystery, this.
There was a woman, once, whose grown son
was tortured before her eyes.
O son my soul,
I observe an agony:
disgraceful falls,
vinegar to drink, ridicule.
Then a nailing to old wood
and total paralysis.
By whom am I forsaken?

Despair is an extravagant word—
part sigh, part shriek—
but the experience, the thing itself,
is a numbness married to a clawing.
You rake your arms.
You rake your eyes.
You labor to uproot sensation,
buried deep.

I genuflect
in the sepulcher of my life.
I kneel, but I do not keen.
Silence is the standard here,
silence and eradicating dark.

Dry

This is a sandstone city built on ash
where ocher smokes
spool upward into ocher smog—
sober pall, snuffing the lights out!

In the crooks of its sills: soot.
In the silt of its milk: chalk.

Thirst. I thirst.
I lift the cup to my lips and taste vinegar.
That's what the spigots give.

The twelve tasks scroll before me.
What is this script?
Coptic? Ancient Norse?
I have no patience for this foreign language.

Take it day by day:
that's the cliché they press on me.
Once I seized the day. I seized the night!
I reeled and was drunk with power.
Now I am weak as a suckling.
My head slumps on its useless neck and I cry for a bottle—
a dry, hacking cry.

Give me, sate me, slake me.
Let me die in my own fashion,
slowly, in increments, over the liquid years.

Hand me the jug, grant me just one swill!
Those who swill, wallow.
Smash the jug, destroy it then.
I would gulp it hollow.

Dread

What is the color of dread?
    Whiter than eye-white, searing white.

What is the odor of dread?
    Sewer gas, a whiff only, quite slight.

What is the sound of dread?
    Sore lungs wheezing.

What is the texture of dread?
    Heart meat, raw, freezing.

What is the locus of dread?
    The tangled human brain.

What is the focus of dread?
    Humdrum human pain.

What is the tactic of dread?
    Dread permeates time.

Child, have you tasted dread?
    On my tongue I have tasted the chyme.

Contempt

It rises in the gorge, yes, it sticks in the craw
and you can't hawk it up, however much it chokes you.
So you live with it,
the gobbet that no enzyme will dissolve,
the sour reflux that no gargling refreshes.
You pencil on a pleasant morning smile,
you squirt a drop of luster in your eyes,
but how do you mask a tenacious nausea?
"What's wrong?" a girl asks, when she sees that smile,
"Are you sick?" asks another.
It's effrontery, their "concern"; they have appalled you.
Just as your boss appalls you: he is second-rate.
Just as the priest appalls you, with his sanctimony,
and the president, with his falsity, hogging the nightly news.

Every day, the gobbet grows larger.
You didn't think you were this elastic.
Perhaps it is having to *be* elastic that spawned it
in the first place?
All that capitulating on the job,
the catapulting drudgeries,
all that bending to another's will?
Or is it a more general buckling —
to compromise, inequity, iniquity, disappointment?
Ach, it is all sourdough,
all gristle, gibbous gelcap lodging in the throat,
gross mass, gross manifestation,
sticking there, in your scuffed craw,
and you can't hawk it up however much you cough
and it clogs the gorge and it chokes you.

A Strange Mazy Life

. . . days a puzzle of tunnels and hollows,
nights a blur of stores underground.
I meander. I ghost myself. Foot follows
foot and foot and foot. A person gets around.
A mind can be maze also: thoughts surge and race,
grizzled rat-shapes nosing their own reaches,
lugging their bulks down this complicated space,
this eternity of halls, walls. Doktor teaches:

Free association! Liberate the repressed!
Let the tongue gibber; the process does the rest.
But I'm not free, spluttering on your narrow couch,
leeching, greedy infant at the breast,
or small blind joey clutching a dark pouch,
intent on getting mine like any pest.

Intent on getting mine like any pest,
I nestle to your singularity
and we are plural, a woman possessed
of a woman, fused in a rite of parity.
Consecration, sanctity! No less
a thing than love is this. I spill, I flute—
my words are fluent in this strange largesse.
But is our bond a bluff, our ardor moot?

That is a thought I shovel under. I will not
quit this captivating passion play—
the plot of it has taken hold of me.
I will not doubt, or compromise what
I have gotten here, though I may
merit hell itself for what I've sold of me.

Merit hell itself for what I've sold
of me? Amen. My loss: my offertory,
lifted on a sacramental plate. I'm told
the damned enjoy inverted glory.
Love, it's glory day when you hold forth!
Your riddles ravish, each a parable
seeding my barrenness. *Once you were cold
ground*, saith the Lady; *now you are arable.*

Somewhere, a woman artist has created
a female Christ upon the cross, voluptuous
in her agony. Many would deface
her, tear her down, but I have waited
all my life for just this image! Pious,
I kneel before you, rapt. You wear her face.

I kneel before you, rapt. You wear her face,
though your face is hardly known to me.
A chair behind me is your chosen place:
relic of the founding grandpapa's formality.
And so I lie here, studying your chaste
decor, your lithographs, your reading.
The furnishings suggest patrician taste,
the books and art a more bohemian breeding.

All day at work I ponder the enigma:
you. All night I map out different histories.
What a gripping journey you have booked me on!
To all my friends I witness your kerygma.
I'm catechetical, mouth to holy mysteries.
What a rare elixir you have hooked me on!

What a rare elixir you have hooked me on!
I'm a junkie, you're my lusted fix.
Each day I skitter the mazes, wild to be on
your couch, feral! See: needle pricks
track my heart. See: infections bloom
in me, and fever. I'm gorgeous with the burn—
and one day will be vanquished by a doom.
I'll thrash, and learn what the doomed learn.

But now I'm well cocooned, mommy's in my bed.
No doom can light, no man can interfere.
I'm snug with you in cozy dereliction.
You are warming me so! You lullaby the dread
right out of me! How well you know me, dear,
to enshrine my past in ritual repetition.

To enshrine my past in ritual repetition,
I am once again a child, your child,
with a child's ideas, a child's affliction—
easily seduced, milady, easily beguiled.
I color books for you, finger paint
my dreams, come skipping to the analytic hour.
This make-believe is bull, you state; it's taint
I was born to. Every giggle masks a glower.

The masquerade is getting out of hand.
I'm tiny now, preverbal, infant, crier,
yowling for your milky consolation,
yearning for your lap, though your lap is banned—
you've abandoned me! You're just a pacifier,
an empty pap, a witch, an aberration.

An empty pap, a witch, an aberration!
Impostor! Quack! Sick money-grubbing tart!
To charge for love is an abomination.
Each month you send a bill to tax my heart.
We've reached an impasse. My failure calls
your competence to question: I am too "regressed."
You shunt me now to other halls and walls—
the office of a Doctor K. It's best.

I cave and I comply. My white eyes
lead me to that other part of town.
The crowds point the way and the foot follows.
Corridors still lead me to the love that lies,
down subways, mallways, brown
days a puzzle of tunnels and hollows . . .

Continuous Play

Shut your pie hole! —
that's the tone I take
with this maddening mind of mine
that won't stop jabbering,
1:00 a.m., 2:00 a.m., 4:00 a.m.,
spewing the day's encounters
into an ear no wad can plug.

It's delusional, that voice.
It talks to people who aren't here.
Everything I've said this day
it repeats back at me,
looping and looping,
blasting like a boom box
set to "continuous play."

And what a smart alec!
It doesn't just repeat,
it embellishes, it improves,
turning even a passing remark
into oratory or poetry.
The people who aren't here
are thus transfixed.

How many other minds, I wonder,
are up and ranting in this small hour,
collaring phantoms,
how many heads thrash on pillows,
wracked by their own noise?
Likely I am some other mind's obsession,
object to be buttered up,
balled out, or dazzled.
Lonely thought, that:
it quiets my own ruckus some.

When silence finally settles,
I'll go under, I'll rest,
if that netherworld of nightmare and agon
can be called rest.

The Unforgiving

To be wronged
is to be zeroed in on
as the autozoom
seizes the image,
as the microscope
homes on the virus.
I have never known
such focus.

To be wronged
is to be toughened
as winter
solidifies water,
as time
petrifies wood.
I have never known
such hardness.

To be wronged
is to be altered
as the vintner
makes wine of the grape,
as the priest
makes blood of the wine.
I have never known
such power.

The Apartment

Let me extol the uses of denial,
imperiled in this age of trite sincerity!
For twenty years, I lived cheerfully
in a fifth-floor brownstone stile.
A blind man, indifferent to décor,
would still have been offended by what scurried
in the walls with such cacophony.
A deaf man would have walked by unaware
but the lurid song of crud and curled linoleum—
that he would have heeded.
Decay invincible!
Denial was needed
if I was to dwell there, and go on.

Denial got me through those years
of squalid dilapidation,
the long unmoneyed years
when having nothing was habituation
and having company was not to be.
But what of the denial of denial?
Now that I have fixed this place
(with what expenditure may be imagined,
with what a fierce activity and hell-bent will),
I can't forget the old disfigurements,
the cracks beneath the carpet,
the sutured integuments,
all the hidden deficits and spackled crags.
They are down there somewhere still,
like crumbling bones beneath a chic old woman's clothes
and she was a poor young woman once,
despised and lonely, scarred, and garbed in rags.

The Holy Name

No name was holier, and none stranger.
It sounded hateful—
that vicious jee, the z-like s, the pus-like *u* and *s*.
Grownups cursed with it
when they stubbed a toe or put a finger to the socket.
They'd twist their lips and spit His holy name.

Even whispering it, I'd quaver.
To say His holy name
was to see Him suffering before me,
for me, His side pierced, His flesh scourged,
His meaty heart all-burning.
How could I love the bleeding god I feared?

Fierce and full of fear is the piety of children.
I had thought I was long done with it

but I am terrified again, and terrorized,
and wild with blasphemy and awe.
I bow my head and warp my lips
and cry a name into this barren dark:
Jesu, I say, *Jesu*.

The Essay

Mother sat down one day with a blank
lined page and filled it fast.
I, who wrote slowly, whose last
college paper took weeks, drank

my tea and watched. The rim of the mug
was chipped, a bother to my lip,
and in the sink, an unremitting drip
discharged its glub and glug.

I set to counting defects all around:
splotches on the buckled ceiling,
scuff marks underfoot, peeling
wallpaper, crumbs in a little mound

between the table leaves. I gulped the tea
and choked on swallowed air.
I sensed an almost measureless disrepair.
Mother dotted an *i* and smiled at me.

In her essay, the season is spring.
Daffodils and tulips "bless" our yard.
Nothing is amiss and nothing's scarred.
She writes of childhood days spent picking

purple clover, plucking daisies bare.
In bare feet she ran in meadows,
then lay and lazed there,
blowing fuzzy dandelions in the air.

And now life's come full circle. A merry
grandson in the backyard can be seen,
puffing a fuzzy dandelion clean:
"tow-headed boy," "brown as a berry."

"But Ma," I didn't say, "he's brown
because his father is a Jew,

and that offended you.
Don't you remember what went down

when Janice married Dan? The fights
around this place, the total lack
of tolerance, and not behind his back,
he knew you hated him. Your essay bites,

it's corny and it lies. Meadows in the weedy
Bronx? Things were different
in your day but not that different.
You lived with seven siblings in a seedy

shack next to the railroad lot
and you slept with your mother
unless your father had some other
plan in mind and you were got

rid of. Tell the truth, for God's sake,
make it real!" But some unthwarted
pleasure in my mother's smile aborted
my literary diatribe. We had some cake

and talked about the seasons
of a human life, avoiding death and sex.
And then we took out the canasta decks.
I've never understood the reasons

for my mother's almost stubborn naïveté
or why she sat down to write
at all, under the buzzing light
of her shabby kitchen, on that otherwise typical day.

The Intruder

The passions in that house,
the rages and hatreds,
didn't shut off with the lights.
In sleep, mother's screams
were muffled, guttural,
the vowels of an injured animal.
Father's were percussive huffs,
the stifled consonants of strangulation.
Into the chamber
of their separate nightmares,
the same intruder stalked.
A boot came over the window sill.
A rifle cocked beside the bed.
Two gloved hands loomed near his throat
or jerked the covers off her.

Over eggs the next morning,
they'd sigh or laugh:
it was just a dream.
No bullet really fired,
no membrane ripped.
Still, no safety came to them.
Day after day, discord.
Night after night, menace.
Night after night, the shadow man broke in.

NIGHT TERRORS HAPPEN IN THE RIFT OF TIME

Between scream and vision, the second splits.
Between vision and scream, eternity.

The pit in the floor is your personal abyss,
the lash of the flamethrower your destiny.

Between the burn and the lit lamp, eternity.

A gargoyle slouches on your fancy bed,
inhaling your exhalations,
vanishing in that nanosecond
between the stopped lung
and the found and fought-for breath.

Are you fighting your own breath?

Tonight, they will materialize,
the warriors in loincloths,
to impale you with Paleolithic spears.

Between the heart hoisted on a spear
and the heart thrashing at a rib, what eon elapses?

What second splits as the viper comes for you,
the mouthparts of the mantis take you whole?

Cinema Verité

An afternoon at the Cineplex
and now the streets perplex
her: such intrinsic art! Faces swim past
in slow motion, horns blast—
the surround-sound
of a city summer day. Drowned
in cinema, awash in its vernacular,
she walks a Broadway studied yet spectacular.
Quick cut: man on Vespa, glasses dark.
Long shot: lady raving in Needle Park.

An apartment building now, a lone
woman wary in an elevator, a lone
woman dropping her keys
at a green door. What she sees
in her foyer mirror, in hard light,
arrests her in the custody of her own sight.

The face the frame has captured: is it her face?
Hue and cry!
She is now what she's long dreaded
unless close-ups lie.

Earthly Use

A saintly-seeming gent with a saintly name proclaims it:
We are more than we appear to be.
Something beyond us shines through us.

I hope I am more than I appear to be.
In the bathroom mirror, the corners of my mouth droop
in an aspect of chronic dissatisfaction
and in the panes of store windows
I've seen my double charging forward
with a bearing of total self-importance.

Yet I too bear a saint's name
and hope to be worthy of it someday.
Even now, at odd moments,
something like air from a bellows may strike me,
evanescent yet measureless,
suffusing me with hearth warmth and light.
Tonight, the vital coal stays cold.

I see God in the eyes of my poodle!,
a starlet on a talk show claimed
and I laughed at her, pleased by my own scorn.
Yet what did she see in her dog's eyes, after all,
but innocence, credulity, docility,
an effortless uncritical craven love—
the typical qualities of saints
for which, thus far, I've found no earthly use.

How I Responded to the Invitation

By not opening it when it came.

By letting it fall behind the mahogany dresser
where it slid with a swoosh into wisps of dust.

By teasing it out, eventually, and holding it up
to the hall's one harsh unshaded light.

By sliding a thumb under the flap
and drawing out
the several glistening paper panes inside.
A multicolor stardust wafted
out of the envelope then,
a glossy stuff which settled on my slippers
and glittered my hair.

By reading it and reading it.

By pacing with it.
By defacing it.

By not responding-if-I-pleased.
I steamed off the stamp on the return envelope
and put it in a drawer with the others.

I am always getting invitations!
All that vellum and glassine wasted,
that precious gold leaf!

Who sends these things, anyway?
Who keeps forgiving my aloofness and my truancy?
Who asks again for my attendance,
requesting it cordially,
calling it an honor?

The Polis of Sorrow

The Polis of Sorrow

How to catalog its infinite occasions?
Sorrow is legion.
Women wail.
Men strangle on their wails.

Children yowl in their beds, if they have beds,
or they are silent, staring, corpse-still—
made so, by sorrow.

In a desert minefield,
along an oil-spoiled gulf,
on the roofs of an inundated city:
sorrow.

And for those who slog through it,
on the other side of sorrow is more sorrow.

It comes as a great wave comes, walloping,
or like a swarm of locusts, feeding,
or it infiltrates like tapeworm or eye worm.

One day you see the worm, traveling your own eye;
one day you feel the woe, gripping you in its pincers.
Cry out or pray or plead: no answers.

There are none to be found here, in the polis of sorrow,
in the vast polis of sorrow, where we reside.

The Washer at the Ford

From a Celtic tale

Young man,
if you must cross the river,
cross it here, at the shallows,
at the place of clear water.
Your piebald horse agrees.
She steps forward
to gulp and be slaked.

Why do you rein her?
True, I am not pleasing to look at,
my wild hair no longer black,
my gnarled hands raw
with all this laundering.

You, though!
You are a big handsome fella —
jaw like a sharp crag at Moher,
honey hair,
a goodness about you like honey.
You've not been shaving long,
would be my guess,
yet you're off a' soldiering.
What war is it this time, then?

On your way, lad.
Don't bore me.
I've no time for questions.
It's better you don't know
whose linen it is that wants washing
or why the water around these rocks
runs suddenly red.

The Stinky Lady

Odd, how someone as small as our stinky lady
can stir up such large controversy.
Even in layers of old clothing, she is tiny,
altogether childlike in size,
though when asked to remove herself
from stoop or lobby,
she throws a child-size tantrum
and that's not small.
Aeaea! Aeaea! Aeaea!
They echo down the block,
the unnerving syllables of her fury.

She favors our building, its warm vestibule.
She rests inside on the couple of steps
behind our glass front door.
I pass her as I leave for work
and when I return from work.
Sometimes I watch her on closed-circuit television,
sitting or slumping, awake in the night, as am I.
Does she ever sleep?
Does she have a daughter?
A doctor, a P.O. box, a welfare check,
anything at all
besides those layered, threadbare clothes?

Somewhere, in some pocket or recess, she keeps makeup,
that rose lipstick she wears, the black eyeliner.
"Gad, I'm beautiful," I've heard her say,
peering into the cracked mirror of a compact.

"God, she's horrible" is the opinion
 of our co-op's board of directors.
They will add more locks
and fine any shareholder who lets her in.
Aeaea! Aeaea! Aeaea!
The feral call will echo not from this place
but from a near place,
maybe every place.
The fact is, I see her everywhere I go:

on 57th Street, leaning
on Burberry's window in her grubby coat,
on Madison Avenue, crouching
on a curb in front of Gracious Home,
and on Broadway, dancing,
her painted face uncanny in the neon glow.
Sooner or later
policemen, doormen, proprietors
tell her to move on.
Aeaea! Aeaea! Aeaea!
Down the canyons of Manhattan
you can hear her wailing.
Aeaea! Aeaea! Aeaea!

The Two

> *In Memoriam:*
>
> *Laden and Laleh Bijani, Iranian conjoined twins, 1974-2003*

Laden, it is I, the other of the two of us.
Are you ready to break free and not be two of us?

Ready, Laleh! Soon we walk alone.
Let's bow in prayer a last time now, the two of us.

Let's ask that Allah lead us through this suffering
and guide the hands uncoupling the two of us.

In single beds we'll wake from anesthesia,
in separate pain and joy. No longer two of us.

To see each other's faces will be happiness.
To face each other! One to one, the two of us.

But if I die, my Laleh, I die willingly.
Let one of us escape the jail of two of us.

And if I die, my Laden, live contentedly.
Live fruitfully, live doubly, for the two of us.

Soon we walk together to the surgery.
Hand in hand, and hand in hand, the two of us.

Early Lessons: Barbarity

Rouge, the tabby who matched my mother's hair,
had kittens in the crook beneath the stair.

Mink Max had hers on the porch, on a perch of dried
cloth. My mother didn't let her come inside.

I was four when Rouge brought forth her litter.
I named each kitten: Sheena, Twinkle, Glitter.

I was twelve when Max grew swollen-large.
She'd purr and preen and queenly strut, garage

to snowy gutter, stoop to alley to back-
yard. And Rouge? Daddy put her kittens in a sack

and drowned them in the toilet. The sack throbbed,
the sack mewed. I held my ears and sobbed

though he said to let them die was just humane.
Max glared at me one day beyond the windowpane.

She seemed untamed, she snarled and hissed and rolled
her arching back. Her newborns: dead in the cold.

I had to see. I let one chill my palm.
I weighed the horrendous news with icy calm

and coldly cursed my mother for allowing the kittens' fate.
Thus it was I learned terror and hate.

When Girls Fight

There were no rule books for girl fights.
It was a matter of pushing, mutual struggling,
our posture almost Greco-Roman, the nobility
spoiled by biting and scratching, dirty play.

There were no lesson books for girl fights.
We were two young she-beasts wrangling in the yard
then grunting in the alley amid garbage cans and flies.
We drove our knees into each other's stomachs.
We shoved.
We pinched.
We scowled.
We yanked at hair.
Joanie's hair was short and wiry.
Her tanned skin bore a horsy gloss
and smelled tar-like, milk-like.
Tar-dark, milk-white, were her eyes.
I saw my own eyes mirrored in their arctic glare.

There were no trophies for girl fights
and no commiserations.
After, in our kitchen,
my mother poured peroxide on my scratches
and swabbed them with Mercurochrome.
She washed my face and tamed me into braids.
Then she screamed at Joanie's mother on the telephone.
She screamed like a she-beast and tore her own hair.

ONCE IN, NEVER OUT

"Little kids, come here! Come take
our scary tour. Behind this door,
a ghost! A headless baby squirms!
A lady—naked!—drowns in a lake

of blood. Gunky vampire blood!
Mummies loll in raggy wraps,
ghouls lurk beneath the bed,
ogres glisten with clammy crud.

You'll get all tingly. You'll shout
for ma, you'll howl and maybe hurl.
No one will save you. See this plaque
on the door? *Once In, Never Out*."

Our Chamber of Scares was a rave.
Linda's room became the House
on Haunted Hill, the Rue Morgue,
the Fright-o-rama, a ghastly grave.

There must have been clatter,
there must have been shrieking.
Linda's dad burst in with fists
wagging. "What's the matter

with you kids, you lousy stinking
kids!" He flipped the light switch.
There we stood, disenchanted,
in an ordinary girl's room, blinking,

noticing his clammy beer belly,
the wrinkled sheet slung on a lamp,
Betsy Wetsy in the undies drawer,
Barbie in her bath of grape jelly.

STARSTRUCK

We defined our eyes with Sophia's kohls,
we glossed our lips with Sandra's tangerines.
We hoarded their pictures, clipped from magazines.

Boys had baseball cards. We had these.
We swapped them in our bedrooms and backyards.
We held them close, adoring them like holy cards

though grace was not what roused us: they lent glamour.
It pricked us with new yearning. Hypnotic pictures!—
hooking us yet loosening old strictures.

Anne Frank, we knew, brought film stars to the annex,
plastering the wall, she wrote, with her collection,
fixing them there for everyone's inspection

but for her own revering too, as saints of hope.
Our plight was not as hers, nor were our minds as fine
but in this one way she was like us: a girl entwined

in dreams of fame and powerful allure,
a girl becoming a woman. We couldn't be sure
but we wondered, as she followed

past the threshold on that siren-blasted night,
if she turned her head for just a second,
toward the photographs, for a last gulping sight.

The Moment

When the Queen of England laments
her *annus horribilis*,
her year of scandal and fire,
I think instead of my *annus mirabilis*,
my year of luck and vigor,
when I caught no cold
and saved and spent
and named myself anew.
Juice, juice—
ideas infused me, and flowed through me.
Then they slowed.
I'd only just hoisted my ladder to the branches
when the fruit fell.

The fruit falls, the miracles trick us.
I was cured of pneumonia once
by a marvelous drug
which germs have since outwitted.
There's small remedy now
for babies yawling with earache,
for sepsis, for the bronchitic cough

and journalists file the story:
plague, pandemic, war
waged with microbes of recombinant design.
The brief age of *salus* is past;
a pestilence draws near.

And journalists file the story:
a great heat is coming, a great frigidity.
Anni mirabili, anni horribili.
The lucky epoch winds down
like an obsolete clock.

Rodin: The Gates of Hell

It is a portal not of souls but of bodies
jammed one against the other in agony
though not in solidarity.
Limbs are torn off torsos, spines contort.
Lips are wide in O's of resignation, not surprise.
So here is destiny, seems the common groan.
What has stalked me in night's shadows has finally got me.

Above the gates, the hanged man slumps in triplicate,
dead on his feet, dangling his dislocated arm.
The other arm points downward to The Poet,
called more commonly The Thinker.
The brawny poet of the people
sits apart from them and broods.
How to divine an unpitying Providence?
How to account for immeasurable doom?
The questions stump him
and will stump him
for eternity.

Hence is The Poet silent.

A clenched hand stoppers shut his mouth.
A clenched hand stoppers shut his mouth.

We Are Refugees

In groups of two or three, we steal through breaches in the mountains.
In throngs, we shamble over trance-inducing sands.

We left our city to the interlopers, with their new weaponry.
We left our village to feral cats and the few dying elders.

We carry dry foodstuffs in woven cloths, and motionless infants.
The Holy Book we left behind, with our intricate carpets.

By this walking we know we live. Do our bowed heads still venerate?
We cannot say, nor do we speak of bleeding or any particular lack.

A little water may flow out of rock; we chance upon a small oasis.
To extinguish a morning's thirst, to move on: it is enough.

There is nothing to want anymore, nothing to expect.
Nevertheless, a child is delivered, ululating in the reeds.

At night, when you fly over, count the holy prayer beads of our fires.
By day, with your instruments, note the many colors of our robes.

We hear from all directions sounds of strafing and detonation.
Is there no place left where we came from, then? None where
        we are going?

SHRAPNEL

After Abu Ghraib

Not to complain, she says, but just to tell—
and keep it down kids, that's an awful clatter—
after suppers now she tweezes shrapnel
out of Vinny's back, a routine matter.

He's doing good, she says, his limp's improving.
He's drinking less and looking for some work.
If all goes well, soon they will be moving
off the army base and back home to West Burke.

The shards will just keep coming, though,
the smoother pellets and the jagged spikes.
She glides them from his body clean and slow.
Going slow is now a thing he likes.

She puts the pieces in a Mason jar
to stow among her staples and preserves,
an emblem right as any stripe or star.
She's doesn't pledge these days, but she observes.

I wonder, cousin, if your Vinny's plight
mirrors in a way these times we're in.
Our nation's coping well enough, all right,
but are we being ruptured from within?

Unceasingly, the souvenirs of terror—
fury, blind vindictiveness, and fright—
lead us into infamy and error.
One by one, the fragments come to light.

The Birth of the Blues

First the seed of the blues,
infinitesimally small,
infiltrates the egg of the blues,
which has been keeping ready.
The process is hidden.
You're not aware of it at all
and for a little while,
your world stays steady.

But a new reality
begins to gestate at the core of you,
a hungry thing,
and it claims more and more of you
until you listlessly walk,
you fitfully sleep;
then an agony overtakes you
and you crouch or weep.

A long depletion follows,
and disquiet in the mind,
and the moment of discovering
what you finally find.
Some say nothing of it.
Some are sounded like a gong.
In them the blues are manifest.
They are become song.

The Cause

> *"It is not necessary to hope in order to persevere."*
> —William the Silent

Some are from the luminous plains,
some from a smog-dark valley,
some from an island nation crushed by tyrants.
No matter.
We found each other.

Together we composed a manifesto
and the preamble to the manifesto.
Together we marched in the capital city, chanting
We shall prevail.

Where we dare not speak or circulate,
we meet in secret, in catacombs, and prepare.

Have you not noticed
the watchwords we've fastened to your lampposts,
the ashes we've tapped into your trays?
Those glyphs in the cornfields?
We made them.
Those runes in the Underground?
They are our mark.

True, we are not recognized much anymore.
Once socialites threw parties for us,
school children mailed us their Lenten dimes.
These days we do not dine so well and funds are scarce.

Hope, too, is scarce.
Our leaders have grown feeble,
there is no young blood,
our numbers dwindle.

Our cause is as much a cause as it was
when we first conceived it.
We hadn't realized

we would face such fierce impediment:
the set cement of what is.

Still, we chip away at it.
In a noonday of despair, we persevere.

We Had Fun

We rode the waves at Assateague,
we let them knock us silly.
We pocketed a sand dollar, and whorled and glossy shells.
We sipped rosé on the terrace, canoodling.
As the sun set, the clouds matched the wine;
we poured more wine.

We had a good time.
We climbed up Cadillac in a lilac dawn.
We schussed down Snow King in a pearly dusk.
In darkness, we whooshed around Space Mountain,
adding giddy screeches to the general yawp.

In Bermuda, in moonlight, we sailed to the reef:
steel drums, tree frogs,
a gooseflesh tingle when the warm gusts blew.
We browsed antiques in Saugerties;
we got there in a spangling car, the latest model.
We visited the last of the Shakers,
buying a doughnut and their hymns on CD.

'Tis the gift to be simple.
Our fun was simple.
Trivial Pursuit on rainy days,
Cheers on television
or America's Funniest Home Videos:
pratfalls at weddings,
pranks in the barracks—
fun.

Fun City was what the mayor called New York
when he closed Central Park to traffic
and soon there were fireworks,
concerts, hot air balloons,
and little red surreys-with-a-fringe-on-top.
The carousel made a sprightly music,

Peruvians piped,
Japanese brides posed under the golden gingko trees.

Those were great days, weren't they?
Laughter came in swells, like the sea.
Ice cream came in three hundred flavors.
We all had so much fun.

There.

Within.

Here From Away

    Do not expect a welcome. People here
are harsh; our inclement disposition matches the weather.
        Our complexions are cracked leather,
    callus gnarls our unextended hands.
    Our jaws are set; we neither smile nor sneer.
You are not welcome, you are not unwelcome, in these lands.

    "From away" is how we'll speak of you,
if speak of you we do. You will agree: the designation
        suits. An old affiliation
    marks your speech and lineates your mind.
    Though you plant a field or occupy a pew,
we'll recognize what's plain: you are not our kind.

    What of that field? It will yield, or not yield.
You own the deed but such a claim is temporary.
        What of that pew, the momentary
    respite from estrangement you hope to find
    there? Certain ruptures simply can't be healed.
Certain quests are futile, insubstantial, ill-defined.

    You quit the bright Cosmopolis to settle
in this other place, this land of sharp cliff and rough shore.
        And though that parting tore
    you at the root, now you quarter into new clay.
    Who knows how long you'll last? You lack our mettle.
But here you are among us, uninvited, from away.

THERE

... where the north Atlantic curls around sandspit
and salts the freshwater,
I walk, thigh-deep: I am almost falling.

I balance on a sharp promontory
as the parabolic wave advances.

I rest with the heron, standing in reeds;
with the three turtles, immobile on a stone.

Do you see that unpeopled strand in the distance,
beyond the estuary,
and the sanderlings darting in the shallowest waves?
I dart among them.

Look down, to where teaberry flowers
and chanterelles scatter their numberless spores.
I think you have missed me, tasting there.

The thump of the woodpecker,
the brash articulation of the chipmunk:
aren't they comical?
Perhaps they receive your human laughter.

The sand is warm where I lay my towel,
the loam under the leaves, a pliancy.
Let me doze a while.

Then I will wade deeper; I'll take an untrammeled trail.
Will you come?

The moon will eclipse tonight
and glow dimly with fire-orange light.
Together we may look beyond it, into the galaxy,
into a torrent of momentary stars.

WITHIN

There is no without here, just within.
Enclosure leading to enclosure.
Less a dwelling place than a condition
and the character of it: contracture,
and the material of it: skin?

Within, within. I've paced it withershins.
I've clambered up its tiny tor and stumbled.
I've fallen down in subatomic spins;
subatomically, I've gotten jumbled.
My synapses are torqued and wearing thin.

There is no delight here, no chagrin.
No down or up unless your name is quark.
A host of quarks can line-dance on a pin
or bounce from Mars to Io to New York.
Or maybe not. No where here, just wherein.

When the Elephants Took Me for their Pet

A grace to be out of that narrow cage, of course,
but when they passed me from trunk to trunk,
they bruised my ribs
and when the female flung me on her back
and went traipsing,
it took all my concentration not to tumble off her.
Did we go east or west?
I don't know if it was a river we passed—
that muzzy brown panoptic—
or a sere savannah.
When we came to a watering hole,
they let me lap there;
the mama knelt and tipped me to a soft ground.

My first impulse? Hide!
I shinnied up a baobab and bucked for a nook.
Then a whiff of something set my innards growling.
Fresh meat: they'd killed a thing
and minced it with their stomping.
Hyrax tartare, oryx tartare—
these were to be my dainties
in the days and years ahead.
I've developed quite a taste for raw things.

I've gotten used to everything:
their nudging me onto them,
their nestling me into them,
their bulk and bellow and stink.
I hardly remember that other world,
the one before the cage life.
It has no substance.
It is like the haze that comes with the harmattan
or the haze at twilight, last light,
dim-benumbing, blur-be-all-ing.

AMNIOTIC MAN

That trickster over there?
He's going for a record of some kind.
That's why they've flooded his diving bell
and drowned him alive in the plaza.
A long tube pumps in nutrients—
hear it thrumming?—
another sluices away excreta.
I'm told he was active once,
thumping and tumbling,
but as you see,
now he's frozen in a body curl
with one hand floating;
no matter how many gawkers tap the glass,
he doesn't rouse to wave it.
I've been coming 'round for days,
something draws me.
Ever watch a goldfish die?

American Highways

Some lead to pasture, some to ice field,
desert, woodland, clear-cut, butte—

this one makes for the clouds.

They are dense and eerily motionless.
One vast amalgamation:
I detect no pattern in it.

Did protogalaxies once mass this way
before their gases were lit by flame?

And the primordial broth,
what of that?—
scummy fusions intermingling
as nebulae . . . .

I can't quite fix my mind on what we're in for.

Condensation fogs the windshield.
Still we drive, we drive.
The ceiling lowers, the white ceiling of cloud.

A Journalism of the Soul

A still morning.

The shore birds are not audible.
The tide keeps back.
One fly, and that one dying,
its lurch like a random tic troubling an eyelid.

I sweep it off the counter.
I do not touch the radio, yet a voice comes through.
The news is war, apocalypse.
Bombs are arcing across the latitudes.
They are the only noise out there —
a high-pitched, alien hum.

I run out to the dunes into a sudden showy light.
I run toward the ocean, I run in my high heels.
How they encumber me,
sinking into sand and sinking into sand.
Panic, a smell of burning: my hair?

There is a cloud tumescing behind Reach Mountain
but I am in the water now, far under the water.
I do not fight for air.
Aquatic, gilled, I have no need for air.
This blue place must be Eden, it contains a garden,
it contains all the scattered pearls.

Oceanic — I am that vast.
No future to goad me, no mortifying past.
Somewhere up there, Terra incinerates
but I have forgotten the land.

I have not forgotten that noonday drowse
when I crossed, somehow, into the soul's locality.
Fear and wish were meshed
and had no boundary.

This is my account of it.
Publish it as special to the *Times*

though it's a crackpot story
and the teller, like the tale,
remains unchanged.

Gulf Coast Gothic

The northern winter got to them: every pore and bone.
They traveled to Florida to get it out of them
and it was warm there all right,
the sun rose and set as in the brochures,
the waters of the Gulf were tepid and placid and green.
Still they were restless.
He left his wallet in a coffee shop and set to brooding.
She got seasick on a tour boat.
Soon they didn't care to leave the hotel.
Silent, on their terrace, they looked through binoculars.
Brown pelicans roosted on brown pilings,
a brown cloud extended a brown claw.
A rum and Coke and a rum and Coke
didn't brighten their mood any.

At last they decided to go somewhere, somewhere marshy
where cicadas would chirrup in dense grasses
and large pink birds would each stand tall on one long gracile leg.
And maybe there'd be wooden walkways
meandering in enigmatic mangroves.
So they took off in their rented coupe
to a place listed in a guidebook:
Amazing Edenglades Evergardens.
He drove; she read a roadmap and watched for signs.
It took longer than they'd augured, but they found the place.

They paid a fee and walked into a maze of pavement—
blinding pavement, shimmying with heat.
There wasn't a flower or a frond in sight, not one fresh thing.
All around were concrete pools the size of wading pools.
Some were painted venous blue, others an arterial garnet.
Lolling in each pool, filling it entirely,
was what you might imagine,
a being with slime for skin and a torpid, hooded eye.
The human couple held hands and stood there,
unable to move forward, unable to retreat.
An atavistic steam closed in on them, a smell like no other,
and somewhere near, a different creature, attenuated, quick,
rattled its enormous cage and shrieked.

In This Church

No vestments or candles,
no incense or statuary.

No missals or hymnals,
no readings or benedictions.

No choir in the loft,
no chime in the steeple.

Pews, yes,
but of what joinery?

Offerings, yes,
but of what coin?

No storied fenestrations,
no gospel or sermon.

Bread without ordinance,
wine without proof.

In the sanctuary, votives:
stubs without flame.

And in the narthex, heels
on marble, echoing,

echoing and diminishing;
slow retreat.

In the Devil's Monastery

> *"Believe me when I say the devil has his contemplatives*
> *as surely as the Lord has his."*
>
> —The Cloud of Unknowing

That inverted crucifix above the altar slab?
How it captivates our heavily hooded eyes!—
the five wounds of the rabbi
bleeding up instead of down, that glib
mouth of his transposed into a leer.
Thirteen times a day we bow and ululate
inside this vault, before this stimulating image.
Rank beneath our robes, we scratch or palpitate.
There is a rite of gluttony, a rite of colonic lavage.

Come walk with me within our murky peristyle.
Carved into this capital: a goat-thighed angel
performing what-you-will on the nude Virgin.
Here Fra Judas cultivates our cloistered garden.
Note the dead man's fingers, cocked at a sly angle,
poking up through carpets of furry mold. Do sit a while.

Now, the Scriptorium. With lapis, egg, and tea,
the master illuminates an intricate *L*,
demons inside it, flames carnelian, home, hell,
Lucifer's Rule preserved for all eternity!

The Exorcist of Alcatraz

A ruin, yes, a dereliction,
but there has been a repurposing.
Inmates of a different stripe
are incarcerated here now.

I am told to steel you
for what you will witness
but you are already acquainted
with the symptomologies and improbables,
are you not?—
Old Nick being a wry one
and no one immune to his skullduggery.

It is my job and that of my confrères
to tease him out of the myriads,
held here, till then, for their own protection.
For your protection, there are these lighted candles,
etched with esoteric runes.
Cup them as you walk
and as you pass from cell to cell,
mouth a paternoster or some other orison.
That will deter the contaminant,
should it be released this day
though it's not a common occurrence,
despite our constant besprinklings and intonations.
For this is less a place of liberation
than a zone of custody and lockdown.
Myself, I've grown immune
to the baleful sounds and smells.
What continues to unnerve me
is the physiognomy,
for no matter whence the possessed hail—
country, cave, or continent—
they wear a single face.

Be ready then
for the stare-down glower of the pinioned clone,
the one countenance.

Maximum Security

*"The Department of Homeland Security will focus the full resources of
the American government on the safety of the American people."*

—George W. Bush

Don't be startled.
That's just your own voice
echoing around the cinderblocks.
You get used to it.
Even the clangor of our iron cages when they shut
mutates into white noise, eventually.

It's crowded all right, new inmates every day.
We don't bother with names anymore,
not with fifteen to a cell
and the constant comings and goings.
At reveille, one or two are clacked into cuffs and spirited away.
You supplant a twitchy little consumptive with a lazy eye.
K, he called himself; just K.

We are fed once a day, one tray only.
X over there is our arbiter,
tearing the bread into portions and doling out peas.
Old timers like myself enjoy our gaunt concavities,
handy for stowing the odd reefer or cigarette.
A certain sentry slips them to us,
asking nothing in return but a collusive wink.
If I believed in an eternal reward, he would be granted it.

If I believed in an outside world, I might yearn for it.
For us, outside is just cracked asphalt,
barbed wire, a few parched petioles of grass.
There is the sun, of course, burning our scalps and retinas,
and the seasonal rains,
and once in a while a breeze
carrying, perhaps, a fragrance we'd rather not remember,
lilac or salt marsh or French roast,
or littering the yard with cherry blossoms.

On such days, we are meeker than ever,

playing no sport, returning to our cells in soundless queues.
How we appear there in the aggregate may be readily imagined:
a thousand stored manikins in a thousand frozen poses,
staring whitely in all directions, seeing what manikins see.

The Carrion Gardens

Welcome to this expo of plushy orchids:
Choke of blooms, the Fingers and Tongues among them.
Stenches on the breeze are their lewd attractants,
rousing the blowflies'

frenzy at their spiky exposed labelli.
To your right, a barren expanse of mudflats
where a pond or rivulet harbored typhus,
drawing the vulture's

claw to beasts who lucklessly came and lapped there.
Heap of bones, the skulls and the sacra strewn there
tell a tale of cryptical ancient epochs,
drawing the diggers,

rat-like people scratching among the remnants.
Now this way: observe an archaic war ground
where the Grecian windflowers fall and perish.
Utterly quiet

but for droning flies and the hissing vapors.
Human bones and skulls in a slagheap molder.
Something on the air from the blowsy orchids—
redolent carcass.

On the Plethora of Visions

You've had a vision, you say?
A great wave stopped in time,
fingers of sea spray pointing their bones at you
as you wigged out on the promontory?
A levitating apple?
A troika of grumpy warriors in the sky?
Calm yourself.
Such things are commonplace—
visitations by neither demons nor angels
but merely amusements cooked up by a bored mind.
The mechanic sees gremlins among the pistons,
the nun lights a candle and the statues dance.
She believes she is touched by God,
he by temporary madness,
but they are merely dreaming.
Something there is that loves hallucinations,
that sets them off at the slightest of instigations:
a dry mouth, an empty gut,
a drop of bitter chemical on a sugar cube.

Oh please stop quaking!
Statistics tell us that right this minute
visions are entertaining millions.
I visited a hermit once,
a naked old man covered in fantastic tattoos
and living under a railroad bridge.
Day after day,
he sees a blue orb tipping and turning
in an isolated zonula of nowhere.
Preposterous creatures inhabit it,
playing games of love and war
and sometimes seeing things just like he does.
It's vivid, that unlikely figment.
So far he hasn't tired of it.

The Architect

I commended Architect for the work he did;
I knelt in his shadow, exalting.
To have meshed the Old Style and the *moderne*—
that was itself a triumph,
and the burnished terrazzo floors,
the baths with their blue mosaics,
the *trompe l'oeil* of the heavens on the refectory ceiling—
these were impeccable elements.
And the corn chapel!
The organic material added leaven to the mix.

I commended Architect for his dormitory of simple cells,
or anyway they seemed simple at first,
but when you looked closely you found embellishments—
little luminous icons, hidden misericordia,
and the beds, though small, were adequate,
the walls so finely wrought they seemed permeable.

I fell asleep in one of the monks' cots
and dreamed a dream about sanctuary
and another that I was dreaming that very thing.
It went on that way, all night and all day,
dreaming serial dreams about prior dreamings.
I woke refreshed, I have to say,
marveling that I'd slept so well and long.
Infinity—
that's where I'd been, and where I'd return.
I cloaked my nakedness in linens
and set to primping at mirrors,
I got on with it,
though sometimes I sit quietly, as now,
to fix my mind, as best I can, on the fantastic cloister.

I praised Architect, excited to be in his presence,
but let me be frank,
the memory of the encounter isn't agreeable.
He neither thanked me back nor raised me high.
The dazzling hem of a robe, withdrawing,
is all I can tell of him.

The Common Room

Romeo's Soliloquy

> *"Hi. My name is Romeo. I'm a canary.*
> *I'm not molting. I have feather cysts. No: it isn't curable.*
> *No: it doesn't bother me. Sorry if it bothers you."*

> *—Lines found on a bird cage*
> *in a Hope, New Jersey antique shop*

It bothers you, all right. Enormous, bleak,
you hover at my cage and rudely stare.
My odd appearance gives you quite a scare.
A bird exploded here; what's left is freak.

My yellow's dimmed, my plumage is in shreds
and like some lunatic I jerk and twitch.
I seem afflicted by some wretched itch.
But do I suffer? Only when your heads,

shaking gravely, throw a frigid shadow
on my sunstruck perch. How you misdirect
your dour pity and terror! You project
on a bird's predicament, human woe!

I peck and peck a cyst, I continue
pecking it: a purpose, a means, an ends.
To be or not to be? Unfeathered friends,
that is a question vexing only you.

Early Lessons: The Quest

Little legs running, little legs pumping—
from living room to kitchen to cousin's room I ran,
not knowing what kept me going,
not knowing, not knowing . . . .

But I was after something!—
some secret that swirled like smoke
between the tweed knees, the nylon shins.
The hushed talk of the grownups made an electric din.
It charged me up, *v'room, v'room,* and I kept going

from hall to porch to stoop and back
through perfume cloud and fog of cigarette
and the phone kept b'r'ringing
and my legs kept ru-running, ru-ru-running

till I scooted to a certain hall outside a bedroom
and a door left temptingly ajar.
So I peeked in!—
and suddenly stood still,
stood very, very still
and glimpsed the secret
displayed, plain as morning, on a yellow spread:

the body of Aunt Peggy on the bed.

RECOGNITION

How tranquil it is, sitting here with my witless mother
who does not recognize me.
I brush and braid her long white silken hair.

When I take her hand, she laces her fingers in my fingers.
Then she sings: *cockles and mussels, alive alive oh.*

She does not remember her marriage of forty years.
She does not mourn the husband she cannot name.
The drunken struggles, the blaming, the carping—
nothing of severity remains.

When a car door slams outside,
she tells me her papa has come to deliver her.
I'll take you home again, Kathleen.

"Kitty has company" a nurse announces, entering the room.
"Company," my mother echoes. "O, please stay for tea."

To me the nurse whispers:
"She acts like a queen, so that's how we treat her."
She, in her commoner's housecoat, a queen?

When her eyes close and her head bows,
we take a nap together in her slender bed.

How restful it is, lying here this August day
with my witless mother,
this mother I prize, and do not recognize.

According to Kitty

Now in the eighty-seventh year of her earthly life, Kitty,
having been settled in an easy chair
and propped among cushions,
was visited by certain itinerant wise men
who wished to assess her mental acuity
for those were the days when it was called into question.
A physician from the village of Searsport
asked her to name her whereabouts
and add the number seven to the number twelve.
A counselor from the village of Castine
asked her to relate the story of her birth and early years
in Capharnaum, or was it Pelham Bay.
A high priest from distant Calais
asked her when she had last received the Holy Eucharist.
Now her answers mystified all who heard.
At last it was asked: Who is the nice lady
who sits beside you, Kitty?
And Kitty gave no answer
but her face was transfigured by a sheer white light.
Whereupon the woman who sat beside her asked:
What is the meaning, Mother, of life?
And Kitty breathed in and breathed out
and seemed to see though she was blind
and clasped her hands into purpling fists
and brought those fists to her bony chest
and smiled a smile full of agony and effort
and breathed in and breathed out
and all who saw these things were sore afraid.

The Common Room

A party today on the lawn of the Haven Manor.
The Elks have sent their rollicking oompah band

and stocked a cooler with colas and cream sodas.
The old ladies have been buttoned into dresses

with white felt poodles fastened to the skirts
and the old men wear cheap straw bowlers.

It's a fine day for staff. They jitterbug
and chat it up with the townspeople.

They don't even notice when Evelyn nearly falls
or when diabetics eat ice cream and cherry pie.

The man who owns the place is up from Portland;
he lets us pose for pictures in his vintage Rolls.

He gives a speech, praising the director
for her valor during January's ice storm

when she kept all residents safe
in the basement of the Church of the Nazarene.

Ruthie and Sam, deaf and blind, panic
in their wobbly folding chairs and are taken indoors.

My mother's tremor has a hold on her again.
She scrunches her skirt and scrunches her skirt

till it's up to her waist and her white undies show.
Nothing to be embarrassed about.

Her legs are as slim and hairless as a little girl's.
She is hairless everywhere and except when she soils

herself, sweet-smelling. I help her into knit slacks
and then into the common room where she sits

on a cushy couch next to her new best friend.
Amy is pill-rolling too; she's pulled off the felt poodle

and weaves it through her fingers. Outside, a wave
of laughter crests and falls. In here, an unlined actress

on TV bewails advancing age and bids us to defy it.
In here, my mother accepts a cup of milky tea.

"Oh yes, that's mine," she says, tasting it,
and sips slowly, sips slowly, every dwindling drop.

The Sureties

Some things you can still rely on.
The Forsythia hedge again is its usual yellow,
the Callery pear exhibits its annual white.
The vernal light is cast as it was cast last year—
Cimmerian, then milky, then bright.
Tulips accrue, woodpeckers adhere
to their nourishing boles, a piccolo.
sounds in the park. Lovers have new grass to lie on.

Some things you can still depend on.
I buried my mother today in the family plot.
Her ashes were housed inside a simple casket—
an easy-to-carry container with little heft,
light as an already plundered Easter basket
when only a couple of elegant eggs are left.
I'd been there before; I'd stood on the very spot.
I'm accustomed to the conditions that lives end on.

Neighborly Elegy

It happens a lot here.
A neighbor dies and you don't learn of it
for weeks, or months.
In the lobby one day, you ask the super
about old Mr. Bethancourt
who hasn't been taking his constitutional
in the 4th floor hall
or you say to young José
How's your mother doing?
and learn for sure what you'd been suspecting
since you'd idly commented over coffee
that you hadn't heard Alba's piano for a while.
How little you knew these people!
You said *Happy New Year* to them in the elevator
or *Nice day for ducks.*
Some you avoided
because they were complainers
or asked how come you gained weight.
Some you favored, like Ricky,
handsome and courteous and robust,
always with his bicycle.
Then he appeared before you one day,
pain-worn and skull-faced,
pocked by a riotous sarcoma.
Now Mattie has died.
For once we find out right away,
thanks to a note taped near the mailboxes.
I know you will miss my sister, it says.
It's true. I'll miss you, Mattie.
Even though you talked too much,
you were a lady, worldly and dignified,
walking tall despite arthritic hips.

I don't believe in ghosts.
That isn't Ricky's Litespeed chained to the banister
nor Mattie's cane tapping the marble step.
This is only me, remembering them,
marveling that I never wept for them.

Island Trail

That red brush vanishing into low brier?
It is the tail of an animal seldom seen.

The heron stands in the marsh grass, as if arrested.
The grass is also still: no breeze arouses it.

No sound in the tamarack, no birdcall, no tizz of fly or bee.
Perhaps the vanquishing sun has hushed them

or driven them to some more lenient clime?
I had not supposed that air could be this cumbrous.

Remember when it gusted off the ocean and whipped the wet leaves?
Gulls with ringed throats raised such brash ruckus!

Azure dragonflies tenanted the cattails,
the fox squirrel showed more than a shy tail.

A dirt path has brought us to pavement, to a zone of defoliated trees.
Exotic beetles have gnawed them bare, or so the pamphlets claim.

This is a long hard trail we're treading.
I do not know anymore

if it loops back to the greenwood
or if it continues in this fashion, barren and irreclaimable.

Night of the Comedians

The first up, he's a dry sort,
hangdog and adoptable.
His one-liners about nothing
take us where we already are.

Give it up for the thin man
with the rufous mop-top.
Not the best in show
but where he takes us we go.

This one enters barking.
It's her shtick,
along with self-loathing
and bitchy send-ups.
She slays for a living.

The Great One pads in next,
his wide eyes glinting with mirth and sorrow.
His existential theme song
brings a tear to ours.
And away he goes.

We never liked this hairless one
with the barbed tongue
but he cracks up the judges
so we chortle anyway.

Daft Aunt Hat will be an antidote,
slapping her knee and yapping.
Then the Strumming Brothers
will come baying in our moony faces.

What a show, the stuff of legend!
There's coke boy, with nosebleed,
high in a gauzy cloud.
There's the freebaser on fire.

The Suicide Memorial

Since you asked, it's still in the committee stage
and the committee often lacks a quorum
when it meets these days
or gets sidetracked by feuding.
Does Camus' qualify?
Should one include Cleopatra's?
Was Cissy Socialite's too tasteless?
They had to scrape her off the pavement with a spatula, after all.

That only *noble* suicides must be honored is the majority view:
Socrates with his righteous hemlock,
the self-immolating monks,
the Christian martyrs who lined up willingly
for the lion's den and the boiling oil.
But a significant few have a fond spot
for sullen teenagers and lovelorn losers
and self-dramatizing poets.

The matter of design is particularly divisive.
A stark reflective wall like Maya Lin's
or something more explicit, like Rodin's Gates of Hell
with its ghastly reliefs and confounding allegories?
The votes are evenly split, the issue is tabled.
Funding has been squandered anyway,
on catered lunches and mimeography and postage stamps

for the committee has been meeting for years now, decades.
How the issue has grown tangled in the interim!
Now, self-slaughter is said to be merely a matter
of brain chemicals, ebbing or spewing or misaligning.
A consultant presented indisputable graphs
and the committee grew apathetic as a consequence.
Valor? Pity? The beauty of human anguish?
All irrelevant.
Why memorialize the unfree act?

And so the committee meets less and less,
especially now that the founding partners,
in their venerability,

are beginning to disremember.
No one's heard from the recording secretary
since nineteen when when.
The whole idea of a suicide memorial
dies a protracted
and natural
death.

Autumn Weekend in Vermont

Rain, a discouraging gray sky, the roads slick and black
and fog shrouds whatever views are out there.
Car trouble now, a haggle with a mechanic,
and hours spent dawdling in a damp town.

Soggy leaf meal sticks to our sneakers
even in the Ubi Sunt antique shop.
They are bringing in the sheaves in that old print over there,
and on that rack, covered with dusty bric-a-brac,
someone's scattered plastic autumn leaves.
"Nature's kitsch" is what you call the real ones.

We've come to see them anyway.
When the weather clears, we'll drink in all the vistas,
the tree-ringed lakes, the calendar-worthy hills—
all the reds in the crayon box, ochres, bronzes, golds.
We'll hit the trails and crunch the leaves
and maybe then our brows,
set as they are in the grim implacability of middle-age,
will finally unclench themselves.

We have lots of company.
The coffee shop, where we order cider and pumpkin pie,
is loud with fellow leaf peepers escaping the hard rain.
The waitresses all dart around and clatter plates—
but one stops at our table to seize a pensive moment.

"I'm so sorry that you missed the fall," she says at last,
studying the streaming picture window.
"I'm so sorry for you, that the peak is over."
"Hot coffee, please." These tidings make me shiver—
though hadn't we really known it all along?
Outside, the scoured maple knows it.
Apprised by gusts, her branches nod and nod.

The New England Poets

In snug clapboard houses, they burn wood for heat.
Chopping wood, piling and hauling, makes them hardy.
They rake and hay, they plant and pick, they put on muscle.
Their poems have muscle too; they are hard-hewn.

In their poems, there are rocks. Rockhood matters.
There are horses, their drawn faces, their quick hooves.
There is an utterance of water, a brook or the ocean.
There is a barn and inside it: a weird, peering owl.

So many animals, some of them lost to us.
Killed by a Boston car or another animal.
Moles, voles, coons, hares,
woodchucks, the pickerel frog.

They chant the genus of each tree in their locality.
They know each bird by its singular cry.
In their familiar wood they stop and listen.
That's rapture, grist for a rugged rhyme.

They pound it out on an old black typewriter,
the words faint for ribbons are hard to come by.
Hard to come by, the solitude that was their element,
and the fox squirrel, the extravagant wood.

Expedition in Mid-life

In my youth,
I would not have climbed
Reach Mountain.
If you had shown me
an arrow pointing up,
a trail marker,
I would have waved you
on your way
then crouched at the bottom,
my body drawn up at the knees
and my head pressed downward.
A starker, more passive posture
you cannot imagine!
Finally, in mid-life,
a sinew in me unknotted,
a debility was righted,
and though it was my body
that stretched up, strong and able,
the healing I speak of
unpinned my amazed soul.

Soul and body, I set out
to climb Reach Mountain
in the August of my life,
in blue-green coastal Maine,
not knowing that the peak I rose to
would be my own peak,
my physical moment,
knowing only
what the squirrel knows
when it scratches its path up the pine,
fleet-footed and single-minded,
all instinct,
all animal radiance.
Under my feet,
the step-stones jutted:
I leaped them easily,
a sylph of the rock,
of the buck and the buckle of rock.

Going higher, I sprang among the ledges
with my primate hands.
Then, from the bottom of the lung breathing,
from the nub of the heel rising,
I achieved the summit,
and looked around.

My descent
was no less masterful:
the way of the coon cat,
capering down,
the way of any object,
even a feather,
when it falls under natural law.
And since that natural day,
that day on Reach Mountain,
a like momentum ushers me along
as I rappel in one ordained direction.
Slowly my strength
—that great endowment—
ebbs. Gradually,
my agilities stiffen.
From here on in,
I won't be climbing any mountains,
only descending,
descending,
but the blisses of the climb
I ponder in my blood
and in the marrow of my spine,
slowly bending.

The Burning Cloud

Why quail? The burning cloud was in the forecast.
Many conditions pointed to its formation.
The season of the supercell holds sway;
prevailing winds have driven it our way.

Many conditions pointed to its formation.
No way to stop or alter it at all.
Prevailing winds have driven it our way
and here it has stalled, in a summer doldrums.

No way to stop or alter it at all.
White nimbus licked by vivid fire! —
and here it has stalled, in a summer doldrums.
Compare: dawn pales, sunset dissatisfies.

White nimbus licked by vivid fire!
Is this the portent of a revelation?
Compare: dawn pales, sunset dissatisfies,
vast fires of the forest dazzle us less.

Is this the portent of a revelation?
Lower your eyes against a fierce supremacy.
Vast fires of the forest dazzle us less,
Pinatubo roars at lesser temperature.

Lower your eyes against a fierce supremacy:
the season of the supercell holds sway.
Though Pinatubo roars at lesser temperature,
why quail? The burning cloud was in the forecast.

When I Am Old

When I am old, if I still see,
I'll kindle up my pixel-book,
enlarge the letters with a click
and read some ageless poetry.

Faithful words, familiar lines
from paper books of years ago
will pass the time at Pointed Pines
or Haven Bay. The screen will glow

and incandescence seize my face.
If eyes be clear and mind intact,
I'll find solace in a bitter place;
I'll find plenty in the midst of lack.

One man loved my company;
no man loved my pilgrim soul:
though griefs may pierce my reverie,
if I can read, I'll still be whole.

And if somehow I happen on
these homely lines on that bright page,
I'll nod in vast contentment then,
however crimped I am by age.

A Man and A Woman

The Keepers

Some new dimension's quickening my room!—
as if some saucy shapeshifters
were peeping out of corners,
closets, dresser drawers . . .
as if the green-clad sandman
hunched and hummed behind the door
and book nymphs, peering up from pages,
recited sonnets to the listening walls.

The bed!
Bold poltergeists conspire underneath it.
At night they hoist a sail
and put to sea
and lift their siren voices
in a chorus—
the sleeper wakens naked,
breathless, thrilled
to feel the eyes
of all those secret keepers
at her call.

What once was a bleak attic,
a chilly stall,
is now an enchanted chamber
fit for a dancing princess
or a suave rich prince.
You're the wizard--
you with your weekends
and your that and this and this.
Today is Friday.
The Keepers know it's true.
They wing my wrists and ankles
as I ready the room for you.

Preparation for the Dance

Across the way, in a city building
twin to our own venerable brownstone building
a male dancer does a spectacular *barre*.
Rubberman, he grips a heel and lifts his leg
to vertical, splitting like a snapped wishbone,
but remaining, by some miracle of sinew, whole.
I lean closer to the glass for a better view,
wondering aloud how the human body can do such things.
It is then that you take me in hand.
Right there, by the unshaded window, you move on me.
You *plié*: our sinuous hips are level.
I *relevé*, easing the removal of my blouse.
Our tongues flick fast *tendus*.
Now we set to floor work,
our limbs bending, our backs arching:
we are tearing apart in our deepest tissues.

Later, I wonder aloud how the human body
can do such things, and do them over and over
like that dancer rehearsing the same moves over and over,
in quest of the perfection of his form,
cultivating pliability, staying ready
for whatever role the company bestows on him.
Maybe, if we keep at it, keep persisting
in this elemental exercise, we'll be ready too—
for pain, for joy, for death's inevitable moment.
Lover, partner, husband of twenty years,
aren't we tireless, aren't we lithe?—
and lifelong practitioners of a right discipline.

In the Key of Snow

In Central Park, you lost our keys,
you dropped them in a drift of snow.
The plows

had not yet cleared the road.
Our boots dipped deep with every step,
hip-

high sometimes, kneecap high
and in the snow you lost our keys.
A haze

suffused the tops of trees,
a *shush* of sleds was on the air.
A pair

of cardinals did not cheep.
Quiet city, muffled, furred.
No one heard

the house keys fall. No one
heard them clink or ring.
How long

it's been since last it snowed,
how long since we were that transfixed,
so lax

that we let go of keys,
lost them in capacious snow!
Awe

is a deep, distracting thing.
We even took a mazy turn,
down

a path that seemed unknown:
it was made over by the snow.
How

long until it snows again
and snow mist caps the whitened trees
and we lose

ourselves, or keys?

Glimpses of the Body in a Modest Household

Enchantment!
I followed my daddy
to the bathroom
and what I saw
so thrilled me
I ran out proclaiming
the good news
to a roomful
of aunts and uncles,
all smiling.

Glee! There
behind the bedroom door—
my mommy with no clothes:
a great tall precipice
of flecked skin gleaming.
O come here, daddy,
I cried, *I have
such a surprise for you!*
And he let me tug him
towards her
and there was laughter
and no shame.

Shame came later.
I grew older
and the grownups hid
and I too was grateful
for long robes,
striped pajamas,
the purdah of Turkish towels
after a bath.

Glimpses of the body
became a worry.
At summer meals,
the rolls of flesh
my shirtless father flaunted
overawed me.

If I came upon mother
unhooking her bra,
I ran from the room,
fear-struck by the oracle
of low, swinging breasts.
And when one day
she came upon me
as I dressed for school,
I clutched the quilt
to my skinny chest
and screeched:
Go away, get out!
Isn't there any privacy
in this house?

And, Love, I am still
a modest person.
That's me at the beach,
camouflaged in cover-ups of terry.
That's me at the gym,
undressing behind a toilet stall.
Still, I allow
your thirsty gaze its fill
and when you walk around
half-clothed, I peep
—incorrigible—
and want to see.

Gaze meets gaze,
again we're blessed.
Such ecstasy!
Who do we thank
for this unasked-for gift,
this enchantment
in which our marriage moors,
this glee?

Florida Love Bugs

A freak of nature—

that was our first impression
of those eerie critters
flying double in the sticky air,
locked at the loins,
swarming around the sun-struck hotel pool.

Our love was new in those days
and our loss was new.
Living together had splintered
our childish illusions
and certain collusions
had levied a harrowing price.

We'd come to Florida
for the absolution of its nodding fronds,
for the benediction of its tropic incense.

We had not expected gospel from the insects!

But the gloria of love bugs sounded everywhere:
a small good news we couldn't fail to hear.

A decade later, we return.
Rapt in our lounge chairs,
toweling our slackening girth,
we smile as a young couple
swipes at love bugs
by the infinity pool.

O Siamese fliers, your sideshow captivates,
you cleave and yet you soar!

Emblems of young love's incessant coupling
and long love's abiding clasp,
someday may you still be news,
cruising by our drowsy heads,
lighting on our weathered wrists,

lighting on the weathered wrists
of all the ancient couples
lying double in the muggy air
in the final quantum of our lives

in buggy Florida.

Florida Palm Trees

. . . those green regencies. We rest easy
under their mild protectorate,
revering a benevolent shade.

Tonight, in silhouette
against a rosy, ermine dusk
they will nod, they will nod.
Our languor will be sanctified.

At the tourist shops,
they sell mini palm trees,
scrawny stalks in thimbles of dry dirt,
packed in cellophane and cardboard.

Feeling foolish, we'll tote one north,
tucked among our shells and sandy T-shirts,
a souvenir as ridiculous
as the queen's image on a tea cup
or the pope's on a plastic spoon.

Still, it will serve a purpose:

To remind us during chill, deciduous days
of how they loomed so regally above us,
casting plush shadows that gave
our drowsy nakedness a holy aspect,
of how we traveled far for this,
their leafy, lush imprimatur.

Sick

To hurl, lose lunch,
pitch cookies,
drive the porcelain bus—
how quaintly we speak of a ferocious seizure.

You are clutched.
Helplessness is absolute.
The world contracts to the size of a jar
and the whole world seems sick.

Helpless, too, are those who watch.
Dry heaves beset them, an incoming tide,
relentless, involuntary—
compassion merged with loathing,
fierce empathy.

What can I do? I called to my husband
as he threw up in the living room,
overtaken in the middle of the night—
but I couldn't even rummage up a pail.
So I pressed my forehead to cool plaster
in the dark hallway;
so I listened.

Tantalizing Sestina

"To withhold the self is not as callous as you think.
It involves most senses.
When your glamour shines, I look
away. When you speak too ardently, I do not hear.
(And when, my darling, you are most tantalizing,
I do not reach.)

I do not reach
because, because—I'd rather not think
about why, I'd rather not consider how tantalizing
intimations overload the senses
so the blood thunders and I'd rather not hear,
the brightness dazzles and I'd rather not look.

I'd rather not look
at dazzling things, whether they are in my reach
or not. And when you want to hear
what I think
of when the lights are out, and the senses
are distilled to touch only, touch, and the tantalizing

ruckus and baubles of dreams, it is not tantalizing.
Why must you strip me of defenses? Look,
it wears me out and shuts down all my senses—
you cannot reach
me, you mustn't think
that I will ever tell you what you want to hear.

This is not what you want to hear,
is it? You want me to say outright, 'Darling you are tantalizing'
and not couch it in parentheses. Think,
though, what it's like to look
away from what you yearn to reach
for, but don't, because you fear a flooding of the senses—

though I admit, the idea of one's senses
being flooded sounds absurd. Hear
how inadequate I am when I reach

inside my gut for you? Tantalizing,
the bayou of the hidden self. So much to look
at there; too much, I think."

No quarrel here. One glimpse can daze you. My senses
have gone under in that everglade. Hear
the tantalizing rustle? Something's there we aren't meant to reach.

Almost

Into my palm he placed a snifter of Cointreau
and into my ear a sexual whisper.
The drums! On the rangy dance floor
I let his thighs touch mine. We got low,
we got down, we slow-danced under kliegs
in that Jackson bar, his mouth on my mouth,
his hands in my hair. Back in our booth
I tongued the snifter, allowing hugs.
Into his car he escorted me. Parked under leaf
we considered: what next? We necked.
I kept sliding out of his grasp, and sidling back,
meaning no tease, savoring what any wandering wife
would savor, after years of quotidian unclothing:
being shaken by an old sweet heat, and taken for young.

That Place

The rightness of it, the gladdening order! A sheen
of waxed wood to walk on, infinite books
to take out of, put back in, infinite niches and nooks.
There is a spice rack, there is a Shoji screen.
No other lives here. So placid. I glide unseen
from room to room, dressed or undressed, my looks
of no import. Here I am whole, here where green
grows the ficus and phones are off their hooks.

The phone is ringing, there's a flood of clutter,
the plants are dry and all the rugs are soiled.
A darling husband leaves no towel uncoiled.
That place where my soul in solitude may flutter
is fantasy. Still I fuel it, keep its clarity unspoiled,
roll my tongue around its substance, richer than butter.

INTO HIS HAND

... cupped in sleep, you'd slip a nickel. Such
gentle stealth: not wrist or finger stirred.
His O-mouth gaped, his snoring chuffed and whirred.
That sly transaction: all you knew of touch.

Double shifts of duty on the subways
conducting a shrill orchestra of doors.
Then tanking up with Clancy's dull-eyed boors.

Back home he'd drop right off; you'd foray
into father's room, bearing your small coin.
You loved imagining him, wealthy-waking—
but did he like the joke? It wasn't spoken.

Today that quiet man lies dead. I join
you, husband, in a rite of our own making:
tucking in his cupped, cosmetic hand this subway token.

Off the Road

When our car, speeding, somersaulted off the road,
I covered my face with my hands.
Light filtered through my fingers in flickering bands.

Something bit my knee and batted my head.
Time slowed, the seconds dawdled, just as others have said.
Still alive, now, this second, still alive, now, this next—

the mind engrossed in flesh,
no boundary, and none between terror and relief.
Infinity and the moment: meshed.

And the car vaulted and it vaulted.
Asphalt grating metal made a harrowing sound.
G-forces assaulted

me, from without, from within,
yet I didn't scream. Like a child cowed at church,
I sat still through all that trauma and lurch.

You screamed. Of that, I was dimly aware.
But you see, my love, with my hands over my eyes
and my heart thrashing, I didn't care

what you were going through. We weren't truly wed.
I learned, that day, that when I die, I'll die alone,
however staunch your vigil at my bed.

The car stopped. Pines stood tall, the sun was bright.
We held hands by the roadside and waited for help
though we were all right.

A Man and A Woman Descending A Stair

It is not a fine stair.
Eroded marble signifies a century of heedless trampling.

It is not a fine place.
Our hard-lit, cracking lobby
spent its *beaux arts* penny long ago.

It is not a fine woman.
Zoë's eyes are hunted,
her figure's gaunt.
She perspires in her puckered T-shirt
and won't stop talking.
Words, tainted by her mania,
spill out in repetitious cant
though it is less a rant
than a plea, perhaps, for sustenance.

She has found it tonight
in the person of this gracious man
who walks beside her down the stair
and up the stair
and down the stair—
for our barefoot neighbor
is unable to keep still,
her willful legs will not stop pacing.

He has found a way
to contain her geyser-urgent energy.
He has found a way
to keep her from the freezing streets.
He escorts her down the stair
and up the stair
and down the stair,
willing hostage of a wild volition,
gallant consort of rumpled queen.

What am I witness to?
I have never seen such patience.
Though his brow sweats and his legs quake,

he remains her faithful cavalier.
He keeps her safe until the medics come.

Ten years have passed, ten years of wear and tear.
Our neighbor Zoë has since achieved
a Lithium equilibrium.
We meet her in the elevator and say nothing
of that night of ceaseless climbing, and nude feet.

Does she forget, husband, your hand at her elbow?
I do not forget.
Watching your courtesy on the stair,
I breathed a silent prayer and I still breathe it
even now, this day,
as we descend that same enduring stair.

Let me keep this memory fresh.
Let it reel and re-reel in my mind like a gripping movie.
Let me be thankful for the company of this man
who abides a woman's frenzy, her mad prattle,
and O Lord, hair-pulling poet or not,
let me be clement with him always.
Keep me from damage, and the doing of damage.
There is tumult in me! Keep it contained.

Supplication

Why smuggle yourself from our rightful room?
Why snuggle alone on a meager couch?
Come back to bed, come lie with me.

An absence has chilled me and ripped me from dreams.
I waken bereft at a quarter to three.
Come back to bed, come lie with me.

At fifty, my mother sequestered my father.
Are we old as that, has it come to this?
Come back to bed, come lie with me.

Though sometimes we toss and sometimes
snore, though passion's not what it used to be,
come back to bed, come lie with me.

Before you know it the time will come
when absence will be a finality.
Come back to bed, come lie with me.

Hope

We've stayed in many towns called Hope,
or New Hope,
we've nibbled cupcakes in their tea shops,
we've drifted on their canals.
We've posed for photos by their old cannons,
their Mennonite stars.
In inns, we've dangled our legs
from their high four-poster beds,
admired their lace canopies,
soaked in their claw-footed tubs.
In Hope, we dawdled over breakfast
porridge and coffee, fresh eggs from the barn.
In New Hope we took a steam train,
in Hope we petted llamas,
in Hope we got cash
from a bank made of Huguenot stone.
In Hope, night fell at four,
in New Hope at seven
and in Hope at nine.
It was full summer,
the trees filled with fruit and a racket of insects.
It was a sound like synapses in the cortex, firing,
or like Salvador, the jungle there,
a sound from Esperanza.
And it was dark, dark.
The only light came from the horses,
the white horses in their pasture,
and the fireflies flickering around them,
a light there and not there,
here and not here, yet reliable.
In Hope, we leaned on a wood fence
and looked at white horses in the dark,
and waited, trembling,
for the next and the next spark.

In Company

Words for a Temp

There are so many risks to belonging!
You can grow fat on the sugars of conviviality
      or choke on ambition's hard-edged bone
          and I've known

    the cloy of one, the slow suffocation
of the other. I glide through my days without
      encumbrance now, a bride of detail—
          no doubt—

    but cool, cool. I give such small
parts of me—fingers to patter their keyboards,
      a voice to trill into their phones—
          and all

    I get from them is something to do
and it's always quickly forgotten: a dull memo
      to "word process" or a chart of numbers—
          I've no clue

    what they mean. It's amusing
to see how excited they get over airy nothing!
      From the desks I occupy, I observe
          their pacings—

    the nodding heads, the hands that pound
the tables and slash the air. On sunny days, their
      dramas play in silhouette
          against bare

    windows, intolerably bright. It's awe-
some, to be sure, but not for me, never again for
      me. I'm no one's food! A steady job
          is a maw

    that bolts you whole, a churning
gut that maculates the soul. I stay clean
      as I pay a transient's tribute to the workaday
          machine.

Green Man

. . . with your green twill shirt
and your greenleaf emblem,
green pail, green tools, green thumb—
when I rummage for evidence
of the humane around here,
you turn up, with your loamy hands.

How mildly you minister to the ficus, the pothos,
the potted ivy in its unsupported sprawl.
Desk to desk, you walk your stations,
crimping and pruning, probing, fluffing,
and humming, it seems, a hymn to Mother Ceres.

Now you take the pulse of my languishing fern,
watering it faithfully, misting its green hair.
I feel my own pulse slowing
as it does in languor
as it might in prayer
if I spent my days as you spend yours,
fostering the green potential of things.

Profit is what I cultivate
in this green building of hermetic glass,
grave and perpendicular,
with the perfect symmetry of the crystal
and a crystal's fine sterility.
Yet your plants thrive
in the hothouse brilliance of the place
and freshen our desiccated air.

And you, green man, with your green garb
and your green touch
and your indispensable green skills
are always welcome here.
We bean-counting bankers happily pay your bills.

Universe Management

In this glass tower overlooking our illimitable city,
a manager mistakes his customers for the cosmos.
I am willing to grant him this one delusion.
The numbers are staggering, after all.
Fifty million people tuck our plastic in their pockets
on this continent alone.
Now consider each customer's "uniqueness"—
how one flaunts our product for prestige
while another likes its value pricing,
another its wide acceptance and utility.
Really there are as many reasons why our product
is consumed as there are consumers,
there are as many reasons why just one will use it today
as there are stars in the night sky!
How to bring order to this chaos?
How to cluster these myriad souls
with their elusive motives
into sense-making constellations
so that our product may be customized to please each user
while our brand, like the sun,
remains fixed and trustworthy and true?
This is the mission of the universe manager.
Ours is named Bob. He does a yeoman's job.

Meanwhile, that other universe expands or contracts,
advertising its amoeboid galaxies
in an infinite medium of matter bright or dark,
welcoming the commerce of the comet,
the flimflam of the supernova,
and managing itself well enough.
With natural law to guide it, it has enjoyed
an unparalleled longevity.

In the glass tower
the manager doesn't think much about natural law.
It's the laws of the marketplace he quails before,
calming himself, however imperfectly,
with the anodynes of research and statistical modeling,

spending his bonuses on cars called Mercury or Saturn,
and continuing to believe, against all evidence,
that his efforts ultimately matter
in this or any universe.

Torpid Transit

On the E Train a woman yawns
and then a woman yawns
and yawns spawn around the crowded car
and many mouths dilate, many lungs swell.

I yawn myself
and gawk into another open throat,
uvula waving.

I yawn again
and watch as heads slump forward
in a heedless doze.

A druggie sleeps on his feet right next to me.
One hand, aloft, grabs on to only air.
He tilts and sways in the harness of his trance
and is held; he does not fall.

At 53rd and Lex, I summon an atom of vim
and exit the car with others like me,
hundreds of other people,
merging in procession, going off to work.

Two by two, on a machinery of looping steps,
we ascend, very slowly,
out of the underworld, into the upperworld,
toward the arousing light.

Our deadpan eyes roll up in that direction.
We fill ourselves with one last Lethe-gulping yawn.

INVITATION TO A BABY SHOWER IN THE CORPORATE LAW LIBRARY

Noreen's day is near. Please join us.
Along leather volumes, brown and black,
we have strung the pastel crêpe.
On the mahogany table: strawberry shortcake,
pink punch, blue grapes, green tea.
Come. Partake.
Join us at the dark table, and revere.

Join us at the dark altar. We'll speak of birthing.
By the leather tomes, with their sterile codes,
we will stake our fertile claim.
Noreen will sit and stroke her ample belly.
We'll plate for her, and you, a wealth of cake.

She will open bibs and rattles, an eyelet blanket.
She will mention the show of blood and the helping gash.
The mothers among us will tell of their various labors.
The childless among us will listen with worshipful awe.
Come worship.

Abandon your desk for an hour. Observe an advent.
Heed a profound and uncodified corporate law.
In this sober place: cake and high laughter,
women, a woman, a mystery, offerings, tales.

Waiting for Elevation

"We are living now in an age of inventions, and we no longer have to take the trouble of climbing stairs for . . the elevator has replaced these very successfully . . . I desire an elevator to raise me to Jesus."

—Ste. Thérèse de Lisieux

This typical morning
as I loiter
with a gang of coworkers
laden with papers
and dribbly take-out coffee,
I too desire an elevator.
Let it lift me
to my cluttered cube,
where I'll hunker down,
efface in work,
succumb to menial offices—
as you, Thérèse,
were once subsumed by yours.
At last a green light, a chime:
we throng into a mirrored cell
and are raised, Little Flower,
to a more lofty station
than you ever could have prophesied.
There, beyond glass,
the sacred spire;
there the bridges,
the helicopter,
the skyscraper,
and all the radiant logos
of our global souk!
It is indeed a dazzling vantage—
but Saint, in your mercy,
raise us higher still.
As we do and are done to,
in the crucible of our humdrum jobs,
give us holiness.
Grant us ecstasy even in dailiness.

TRAVAILELLE

We work in joy or rue.
We earn a bit, a lot.
We drown in what we do.

Outside a cosmic view
dwarfs us to a dot:
we haven't got a clue.

We dare not look. A few
may look. So few. So what?
We drown in what we do.

The holy sages knew
that getting's a garrote.
We haven't got a clue.

We get and spend and woo.
We want: a dhow, a yacht.
We drown in what we do.

Is there a path more true
to some more ample spot?
We haven't got a clue.
We drown in what we do.

After Long Days Visiting the Nursing Home, I Return to the Office

. . . to screen calls,
take minutes,
tweak numbers,
draft, deal, fax,
fix coffee,
smile the robotic smile.

How well everyone seems,
gesticulating forcefully,
walking unfalteringly on sound legs.
No one says *fork* when he means *briefcase*,
no one snores at the conference table
or slumps limply at her desk, dribbling.
Our chairs have wheels
but only so we can work faster,
swiveling deftly in the direction of tasks and purposes.

Odd, then, that breezing by a certain open door,
I catch sight of Manny, in his shirtsleeves,
motionless, emotionless, corpse-eyed,
no purpose in his eyes at all.
I hurry by
but sidewise I perceive his silhouette,
faint behind a scored glass wall.
His head is in his hands now,
his spine bows,
his weary posture an augury of times to come.

The Triumph of Eros

In a bull market, a depression grips us.
We shamble to meetings with drooping heads,
we wear a plain and shapeless garb.

We are like monks, practicing custody of the eyes;
like nuns, shunning "particular" friendship.
Eros must be vanquished for the common good.
It says so, right here in the employee manual.

Perhaps Peg and Don haven't read it
for I spied them today, necking in the copy room.
Peg will soon be fired, if past experience repeats,
or one will be sent to Brussels, the other to Albuquerque.
One way or another, the situation will be "handled."

I worked once in an old loft building, plagued by mice.
We kept cats around to hunt them—
two neutered tabbies, fat, snoozy,
more unsexed than the drabbest of company drones.
Yet I came upon them one day, coupling on my boss's desk,
rumbling and yowling in feline transport,
shedding all over his blotter and lawyerly files.
I shut the door and left them to their shameless offices.

High Floor Ballad

Raise the shades, let fog reveal us
        even as it blinds.
Shut the lights off. Turn the phones off.
Hush your chattering minds.
        Hush your chattering minds.

Stand before these opaque windows.
        Something may be seen.
Press your cheek to the delicate glass.
Press your palm there. Lean.
        Palm there. Press there. Lean.

Gaze into uncanny dimness.
        Gaze into the gray.
Within the cloud, unknowing blurs
into a clarity.
        Into a clarity.

Raise the blinds and take the cloud in,
        breathe the absolving haze.
Let it inform us, let it suffuse us.
These are the lucid days.
        Breathe the absolving haze.

A Roadblock in the Negotiations

When it happens, it happens after hours.
Discord in our midst. Baring of claws.
What have we done to raise daemonic powers?

Undone, a good day's work! What devours
the crumbs we threw, concessions to the cause?
When it happens, it happens after hours.

Fatigued, we clash with bitter words and glowers,
in thrall, it seems, to elemental laws.
What have we done to raise daemonic powers?

Why not settle? Must we clutch what's "ours"?
A matter of fate, perhaps, of human flaws?
When it happens, it happens after hours

as patience flags and interdependence sours.
This force discomfits even as it awes.
What have we done to raise daemonic powers?

So we are stuck and slump like wilted flowers.
Agreement nears, then teases, then withdraws.
When it happens, it happens after hours.
What have we done to raise daemonic powers?

Love and Work

They say it all comes down to love and work.
Our lot: incessant dance of love and work.

We build, we serve, we cling, we yield,
we give, we're given over: love and work.

The dance exhausts. We're strained and pulled apart,
injured and used up by love and work.

The dance elates, arouses, lifts us high.
We're spry. We strike a balance: love and work.

Or if we trip we still go reeling on.
Jobless, lacking mate, we love and work.

But does it all come down to love and work?
The lilies of the field don't love or work

and yet, O Lord, it's said you tend them well,
who merely are, who do not love or work.

After

You were sure you packed everything—
family photographs, your Steuben paperweight,
that extra pair of shoes—
yet you rummage through the deep carton,
clawing at tissue, popping bubble wrap.
Something is amiss and something's missing.

Here's the company phone book and there your name in it.
Here's the silk scarf that was your parting gift.
Did they really picture you in lavender and white?
Pastel is what you are to them now, perhaps,
and them to you, a watercolor viewed at a distance
through memory's filmy eye.

Already you forget the name of the mail clerk,
and the access codes, and what it was, exactly,
that made this severance seem shrewd.

You had thought you were paying attention!—
but you were dreaming.
The place was a virtual reality,
absorbing, beautiful even, but strange,
the skyline views both vivid and vertiginous,
the corridors labyrinthine.
You flew down them as if in free fall.
What was the urgency?
What have you lost?
What will you do with this dusty stuff?

In Company

After two years of writhing solitude
I come back to the crude
arena of the living, to take my place
at a front desk, arrange my face,
and welcome callers to a fabric
company. Nearby, my pick
of seven beds, each arranged
with the firm's designs: deranged
ferns, bulbous roses,
cats, dogs, in supplicant poses.
On sleazy 32nd Street we show our wares.
In the back room, six artists share
four drawing boards and are forever
quarreling. Allegiances sever,
complaints are croaked into the tainted
air. And still the hideous patterns are painted.

When the chairman has a heart attack
and the glamorous design chief gets the sack
and the artists finally blacken
one another's eyes, I do not slacken
off as once I might have. Instead
I am alert to chime and phone, wed
to the work as a honeymooning bride
is wed to untiring ecstasy. Oh, I tried
the way of the anchorite and became
no purer than I'm becoming in this game
of argument and hustle and stale woes!
If my calling be to hawk the garish rose
then I accept my calling. To be
imperfect and of use is all I ask: to be
        in company.

The Transformation

We couldn't say when it started exactly, the transformation.
Interoffice envelopes began arriving
with our names in fine calligraphy: that was an initial sign.
Then a young manager gave a presentation
using words like *gouache* and *crescendo*
and the bullet points on his overheads
were like icons from the Book of Kells.
Soon after, we stopped ordering platters wrapped in cellophane,
favoring delicate quiches instead, or an array of soups,
or sushi delivered by a tranquil gent
who set our conference table with a studied reverence.
Our divisional vice president cultivates orchids now,
our receptionist displays pots and pots of African violets.
We set aside days for cultural celebration
when the office is a panoply of turbans and kimonos,
kilts, saris, dirndls and dashikis.
Other days we all wear an item of like color, or white.
Sometimes a hush settles over the crowded cafeteria,
the cacophony dissolving into a great silence.
And just this morning, our companionable computers
booted up with the tinkling of Zen bells.
A message materialized on every screen:
We have gathered here today to engage in joyful livelihood.
Let it engage us entirely, that we may be enlightened and fulfilled.

Lovechildren

LOVECHILDREN

My children all have different fathers.
Mom's prolific, blowzy, loose.
My children all have different mothers.

Bikers in their bad-ass leathers,
priests and mystics, Vulcan, Zeus:
my children all have different fathers.

Moods are like unstable weathers;
masks come in and out of use:
my children all have different mothers.

All those mothers! All those others:
bedroom moans of bliss, abuse.
My children all have different fathers.

Bride of seven bastard brothers,
seer, hooker, clerk, recluse:
My children all have different mothers.

Motley brood, they share each other's
scandal as I reproduce.
My children all have different fathers.
My children all have different mothers.

The Forgotten Prophets

"...we tend to remember only the prophets who turn out to be right."
—*Joseph J. Ellis, Founding Brothers*

Let's *not* forget the bungling prophets, those
who guessed a Persian win at Marathon,
a Greek one at Thermopylae, or in the court
of T'ai-tsung foretold a feeble, short
ascendancy for Empress Wu. Even the Sun
King staked his bets on harebrained auguries!
His cocksure war on Holland was a dud.
They breached the dikes and routed France with flood.

Let's wonder how the hapless prophets fared.
Perhaps they fell on swords, got locked in stocks,
were paddywhacked from canton, court, or town.
Cornwallis's, I hope, was somehow spared,
who told the bloke, "No sweat. You'll clean their clocks"
and tipped the old-world order upside down.

What Goes Around

These two accuse us: we have dinged their car.
You parked too close; I bumped them with my door.
What once was new and perfect bears a scar.

We two stay unresponsive. Suspects are.
But dodging blame just makes them rant the more.
These two accuse us: we have dinged their car.

At least there are no feathers here, or tar,
or witnesses whose laser eyes might bore.
What once was new and perfect bears a scar.

These two will not back off; they want to spar.
They want us sorry. Their aspersions roar.
These two accuse us: we have dinged their car.

They make us scrutinize the fugly mar
and screech that there is nemesis in store.
What once was new and perfect bears a scar.

They mean that what goes round on this blue star
comes back around again. Portentous lore!
What doom awaits us then, who dinged this car,
who spoiled its new perfection with a scar?

The Spell Weaver

From the life of Edna St. Vincent Millay

Daughter, said Mother,
I know what you do.
I know the charm of it.
I was young too.

I've watched you at mirror,
brushing your hair,
touching on perfume—
there, not there.

Whirling and posing,
a feverish sprite,
running downstairs,
seizing the night.

Drowsy at breakfast,
your cup at your cheek,
your peignoir disheveled—
no need to speak.

No need to tell me.
I see what I may.
I see you're in trouble:
the family way.

Come off to Dorset.
We'll tramp around towns.
We'll husband the thistles.
We'll walk up the downs.

And so to Dorset
the two of us went,
flushed with an ardent
unuttered intent.

Days on end
she searched the fields

and studied an herbal
and stole away yields:

Henbane, hyssop,
heal-all, mallow,
clover, nettles,
hawthorn, yarrow.

At the wood stove
Mother toiled,
stirring and brewing.
Tonics boiled

and filled our shack
with an alien fog
and filled my throat
with a smothering clog.

But oh, how lovely
Mother looked
whenever she measured,
whenever she cooked.

June progressed
to lush July.
A new thing blossomed
by and by.

A new thing Mother
had to get.
Favored of Venus:
alkanet.

Its leaves were furred
and made a flare.
Its roots were redder
than my hair.

Red the tincture
Mother brewed.
Wyrd infusion!
Witch's food.

I drank it fast.
She took my hand.
We walked all day.
A struggle to stand.

Sore to my marrow,
weak to my toes.
Sometimes I retched
between the throes.

Mother stayed near
and held my head.
She gathered leaves
to make a bed

and by and by
she took a cloth,
spat on it,
and wiped me off

and told me please
Do not look
as she buried the cloth
and buried the book.

And when I opened
my shuttered eyes,
sunset burned
in Dorset's skies.

Splendid with youth,
gorgeous with might,
Mother glowed
in that red light.

The Ritual

You ask how many years we have gathered here,
at Clan Rock, to conjure the dawn sun?
We summoned the first sun.

You ask the meaning of our chants and gestures
and what our feet are spelling
as we thump out these thundering percussions?
The ancestors knew.

Our customary number,
seven times seven of us,
seven times circling,
seven times blowing the whittled reed,
with its seven perforations?
It is not written.

This glitter in our eyes?
It is the mark of absolute power.
The moon pales.
We have authored day.

Should we linger on our mats one night,
should just one choose the work of dreams
over this more necessary work,
what would come to pass?
Why, we ask in turn, would we risk disaster,
baleful darkness, earth denied all light?

Money: A Valediction

Coins, farewell.
We pile you up no more,
nor wear you down with rubbing.
No jangle in the pocket,
no clink in the hollow bank.

Dollar bills, goodbye.
So long, crisp crackle,
fat wad in the wallet,
provocative folds in the clip.

Cash, you are old currency.
You no longer register.
We tender with plastic now,
with magnetic bits in chips;
even our retinas soon will be capital.

Where have the presidents gone,
who lent you such decorum?
Where are the monument and the torch?
The buffalo, where is it roaming?
The Latin motto, so esoteric,
who does it confound?
Who utters anymore the confident prayer?

Only in memory
does the pyramid cleave and glitter,
its immense eye staring
in redoubling dark.

Salvific Ode

I would praise what saves us,
through assaults and shamings, what saves us.
Through ridicule, and violation.

A boy is mocked. It is the custom here—
the body all wrong or the speech peculiar.
He endures. What saves him?

A girl is slapped in front of others.
Look: the mark is on her, indelible.
She moves on. What saves her?

School: odious echoes and memorization,
coercive, diminishing, dull-eyed, robotic, and rote.
Still many learn. What saves them?

Home: constant intrusions.
Pryings and enemas,
fault-finding, blaming, disgrace.
No escape, yet the child is saved.

I praise what saves her
I praise the flint of her secret will: small spark.
Where terrors would infiltrate: small spark.
Among the desolate and the injured: small spark.

Next to an outhouse in a weedy park,
in the despairing shade, in the rubble,
the lady's slipper dangles, cèpes drip,
green jack tips in a green pulpit.

SOCIABLE ODE

Cocktails, a mahogany bar,
men in crisp suits, women in high hair—

a glare
of glasses hoisted up in toasts:
toasts everywhere.

And everybody jokes.
And everything you say is sheer
beguilement. And everything you hear

is razzmatazz, vivid-
ity! Oh, every cheek is in high flush
and every mind has rid

itself of stricture!
Work is over; this is play,
a sinuous, furious leisure.

This is interplay,
a witching hour: quick wits
charm the way

to giddy and giddier enchant-
ments. What a wicked spell!
Even I, who usually can't

be glib, *am* glib
to a fare-thee-well,
full of quip and rib

and scintillating riposte.
Hand me the snifter,
now I make my toast:

Here's to good talk and good looks,
to sexual sorcery after dusk.
Here's to our human laughter, our animal musk.

Rienelle

> *"I have nothing to say and I am saying it in poetry."*
>
> — John Cage, Lecture on Nothing

No meaning, no import, no point, no wit.
I speak of nothing, not even weather.
I've nothing to say and I'm saying it.

No thoughts alight. They drift or flit.
I bring no focus. I'm not "together."
No meaning, no import, no point, no wit.

No sense whatever, not a whit.
No reason why I say "bellwether."
I've nothing to say and I'm saying it.

I yawn, drum nails and squirm a bit,
hum tunes of edelweiss or heather.
No meaning, no import, no point, no wit.

A pen without ink, a fruit without pit,
a joke without pith, a wing without feather.
I've nothing to say and I'm saying it.

I probe a nostril or pick a zit.
Boredom is my choice and tether.
No meaning, no import, no point no wit.
I've nothing to say and I'm saying it.

Light on Water

> *"Darn near impossible to describe the effect of light on water."*
> —A problem articulated in a poetry forum

Slippery beam, rippling.
                Liquid luster, sparking curvature.
        Unpinnable, elusive:

        dawn's reappearing blush,
                dusk's disappearing glint.
      Glitter at noon, blinding.

Flickering candlelight of moon
                distracting Ahab from his quest,
    Ulysses from his destiny.

        Eerie glare,
triggering migraine, epileptic fit;
    hypnotizing the skeptic,
            mesmerizing the cynic.

Light and wave, shifty as Proteus.
    Like Brutus, devious.
        Bracelet of a goddess, many-armed.

            Poseidon's firework,
    ocean's filament,
        tiara of the frigid mountain tarn

    adorning too the Persian Gulf,
        the Great Salt Lake,
this humble and transitory puddle

        from which I've plucked
    a glowworm
coiled in undulating light.

The Widest River

It's the Seine, if you're in it,
if you've bounded off the *Pont du Carrousel*
to save a drowning woman
and strong currents pull you in the wrong direction
and your saturated clothing, your fine worsteds and silks,
make each stroke and kick a difficult toil.
You don't feel like a hero at all
but like a victim, a victim
of that careless woman who has fallen in or jumped,
who might grab your ankles at any moment
and haul you into the filthy, frigid water.
How angry she makes you —
but then you remember
her lamplit face as it went under,
it's your beacon, and you press on.
Later that night, at the Embassy banquet,
you will kill the taste of river scum
with fine smokes and wine
and say nothing of the rescue.

So it is with the reticence of heroes
and so their exploits go.
In the cancer ward, a nurse wipes off a patient's puke;
she's tender, though she's sickened by the smell.
In the twin tower, a fireman climbs and climbs,
wanting to be anywhere else,
anywhere but in that endless stairwell
with his deep bone's ache and his bulky equipment.
Whether he does his job well today or recklessly, he may live;
whether he forgets himself or pities himself, he may die

as Eugen Boissevain might have died
but instead he lived, to tell us, by and by,
of how, on the night of the Embassy banquet,

he sprinted from the haven of his limousine
and leapt into the pestilential Seine,
of what a nuisance it was to be gallant,
what a drudgery and bother,
and of how, if it came to it,
he would dive into the blackness once again.

Atlantic City Idyll

Come bet with me and be my luck
and bring me gimlets tart with lime.
We'll chase the wily holy buck
and toss the dice and sneer at time.

Oh, we will dazzle in our clothes
and neon dazzle us as well.
We'll strike a sleek and moneyed pose,
we'll yell a blithe, ecstatic yell

until at last we've squandered all,
shot the wad and maxed the cards,
until we've quaffed till dawns appall
and hoarse are velvet-throated bards.

Come stroll with me and be my muse
of feckless hope and vain desire.
On the boardwalk the huckster woos
and Armless Annie tongues her lyre.

The Awkward Age

Ungainly years of stammering and spills
when nothing seemed to fit, not limbs or nose!
Smells abashed you, inconvenient flows.
With those you loved who loved you, you clashed wills.
With those you feared who mocked you, you allied.
Or else you joined a different, wayward crowd—
strength in numbers, cow them or be cowed—
though some escaped in books, or suicide.

I'm told all life derives from primal sludge,
atoms made cells and cells evolved to us
and if we stay the course we'll still progress.
Our hot antagonisms will flare less
until we're louts no more, or mutinous,
or bear our kind an adolescent grudge.

The Sociability of Nations

Let nations bow to one another,
let them tip their many silly hats
and shake hands.

Let them call on one another,
pour each other Assam tea,
offer a Cuban cigar
or a Belgian chocolate.

Let them take each other touring
in a Maserati or a Subaru
to view the great Kula Kangri or the Great Plains,
to photograph each other's ruins,
to gasp at bald eagles, penguins, cockatoos.

Let them roll around a soccer ball, a golf ball, a bocce ball.
Let them play mah-jongg or Crazy Eights
or Intellectual Botticelli.

Let them entertain each other
with flutes and santoors and steel drums.
Let them sing *There's Whiskey in the Jar*
and *This Land is Your Land*.

Let them put a shrimp on the barbie,
a goat on the spit,
let them camp together on Omaha Beach
or in Plitvicka Park
or in the Serengeti, by a magnificent rain tree.
Let them tell folk tales by the fire
or a couple of elephant jokes
as the moon wanes or waxes or eclipses.

Let them escort one another
to a White House dinner,
a long house banquet,
let them wear Armani or batik,
jade or pearl or tourmaline.
Let them toast a year of world peace

with the world's finest wines.
Let them relish the *amuse bouches*
and the appetizing crickets
and then belch loudly with a studied etiquette.

To celebrate the birth of a constitution,
let gifts be sent, crystal paperweights, historic quills.

To commemorate the end of a chronic war,
let monuments be draped in purple silk.

And when Pax Mundi is somewhere broken—
for peace is fragile and will be broken—
let every nation recognize its own body as broken.
The body will rally, the wound heal.

This is my vision, however naïve, however utopian.
I hold it out to you,
though you will not grasp it in your lifetime.
For now, come walk with me in my damaged city.
It is spring now, 2002 in the common era,
and one million daffodils bloom
in one million tiny plots of soil.
They were given by The Netherlands,
a nation that cries with us,
and dreads with us,
and sends flowers
as a friend will when a friend ails.
They are everywhere you look.
They are so richly yellow, so terrifyingly delicate.
They light this darkness with their perennial gold.

THE FROZEN SEA WITHIN

> *"A book must be the axe for the frozen sea inside us."*
> —*Franz Kafka*

I too took up the task. I raised the axe
and brought it down into that sea of stone.
I worked hard. I didn't dare relax
though every stroke exhausted every bone.
Harsh hours passed, and weeks passed: time careered.
Still I carried on my occupation.
More ice would form as soon as ice was cleared.
Still I had at it without cessation.
      Slavery at my own hand, violence!
I stopped my toil, shuddered, pitched the hated
axe into the wind! And then I drowsed. Dense
dreams unburdened me. I roused. Yawned. Waited.
And see: the season changes, the sun creeps
to noon. The sea is melting. The dolphin leaps.

Nothing.
Not Nothing.

What Pervades

Fog pervades the whole northeast this morning.
Shades are drawn but still I sniff the steam of it.

I waken late and look up into gray bewilderment.
A saturating haze arrests the mind.

I breathe an air that seems as thick as chrism.
I grope and stagger in a tugging undertow.

It excites me, almost, the inexorability—
a heavy down-pull like a joyride's g-force.

I raise the shade and peer into a cloud now.
Vagueness, darkness. Nothing can be fastened.

God is nothing, God is not-nothing utter the sages.
What permeates all being leaves being all alone.

No hiding from this vapor, however it hides.
Fog pervades but what pervades the fog?

SHE

> *The Shekhinah . . . is supposed to be everywhere,*
> *and it is exile that carries it everywhere.*
>
> —Elie Wiesel

On the banks of the Ob, at the source of the Nile,
in a curtain of reeds, she wanders.

She raises a lantern: its flame is extinguished.
She stumbles. She reels. She wanders.

No clatter of pebbles beneath her sandals.
Where night jasmine opens, she wanders.

Heat lightning flashes her dark silhouette.
Through sandstorm, in snowfall, she wanders.

She stops. She weeps. She swivels her neck.
She pulls at her garment. She wanders.

In fog, in mirage, in a forest of cloud,
in vapor of marshes she wanders.

Night is her element, exile her destiny.
Everywhere, nowhere, she wanders.

Ever since, beyond, unto, always, until, she wanders.

Self as a Refuge

Variations on a teaching of Theravada Buddhism

Make yourself a refuge: there is no other refuge.
Intruders will crack the strongest lock.

Typhoon will sink the soundest watercraft.
Make yourself inviolable harbor.

Divest of excess. Dearth is also treasure.
Robbers do not loot the empty coffer.

Hooligans may sack the mountain cloister.
Be in the world, then: bide in shadow cloister.

Otherness may mark you, some will shun you.
Be undisturbed: forbearance, your asylum.

Be tabernacle, ark to timeless Presence.
Be sanctuary, chaste and ample space.

Dust and Sin

A useful and quotidian perdition
has choked my home in strangleholds of dust.
My throat and lungs have borne it as they must.
Refurbishment's achieved by demolition.

Dancing dust motes—angel dust—beguiled
me in a church once, in a shaft of light,
transfiguring my penitential fright:
I was a guilty, visionary child.

I am a dreamy, guilt-accustomed wife,
mindful always of a taint within:
the residue of some intrinsic sin,
the dusty nature of my hidden life.

Through my most grievous fault, we prayed
at Mass; self-loathing seemed the saintly mark.
I'd quail before the most benign remark
in those days; the quailing habit's stayed.

And now this dust besets me, a fine silt
on surfaces, in corners, underfoot,
not a common house dust, more a soot,
a Vesuvian ash where corpses never wilt

but lie for eons in amazed repose,
arrested in a past in which they froze.

The Incompetent Mystic

. . . braids his legs, stands on his hair,
chants, bows, eats his bowl of air
but can't stop fingering his jutting bones,
they have such delicacy.
He names them:
scapula, sacrum, tarsus.
They tie him to this flesh, this world.

He is tied to this world by many things:
Kali dancing, Shiva dancing,
Vishnu the lion-man, the boar —
the fascinating idols hold him.
At his feet, idolaters charm him —
the boys with their long lashes,
the girls with their ripening breasts.

They come to him for wisdom;
he hasn't the radiance.
They come to him for healing;
he hasn't the touch.
The crippled do not walk,
the leprous are not cleansed.

Attachments obsess him:
prayer wheel, mantra, saffron robe.
Folded in his hem
he keeps a picture of the globe,
the planet seen from space,
rising at the moon's austere horizon.
Perhaps there is only one god after all,
he thinks, knowable only
by those omnific oceans,
those jigsawed continents,
that sheer sari of clouds.

But he is pledged
to gods of void and bliss,
transcendent, utterly other.

Again he fasts, again he sits,
again he chants and sits and sits,
and fails to flee—
for he counts his bones—
earth's tether.

The Elderly Atheist

I've got a spring, still, in my geezer's step
and, yes, I carouse on Sunday—
golf and smokes and booze—
and still don't join in grace at meals
or deign to pledge allegiance.
God is for simpletons!
I decided that in tenth grade and haven't wavered since,
not even when, in trying times,
my fellow rascals fled, quaking, into pews and truisms.
Ultimately, they preferred the canned answer.
Myself, I favor science with its testable proofs
and ceaseless self-corrections—
the real *aggiornamento*, no?
The rational, updated way to live.

The soul?
Bonehead notion, where do you find it?
Spirit? Ditto.
Solace? No need.
Can you not accept this life of ours,
its slapdash tribulations?
An afterlife? Listen.
For years, I watched my wife disintegrate
right here in Dutchess County
until she had no memory at all.
Fifty-five years of marriage, erased,
her childhood summers at the lake, extinct,
the cloud of three miscarriages gone from her eyes
along with gaiety and self-awareness.
I leave it to you to deduce what may be kept in death
if you can lose that much in life.

I've lived a long time without faith or hope, young lady,
and I intend to die without them
I've willed this parched carcass to university hospital.
Someone much like you will peel my skin
.

and probe each worn-out nerve and sinew.
She'll dissect my balls
and wiggle my arthritic finger bones.
Let her have her spree.
I won't be watching, I won't be not watching.

Sister Rigor Mortis

Oh, the times! Oh, the situation!
We who hiked our uniforms above our knees
and called communion wafers "corpus crispies,"
will you forgive us for the appellation

we gave you? You stood so rigid and erect
as you declaimed a Cicero oration.
You were so old and tall, no coloration
vivified your cheek. Wasn't it correct

to dub you Rigor Mortis, Latin name
for "stiffness after death," wasn't it wry?
Didn't it suit you, didn't it apply?
That it might hurt you was a thought that came

and went. If it hurt you, you never said.
You loomed at lunch or monitored the hall.
You made us translate "Love conquers all"
and bored us silly. The language was dead.

Who cared about datives, or the three parts
of Gaul, or if the die was cast? Who cared?
Still you taught us, who mutinously stared
you down and mocked you, whose barbaric hearts

would not be taught a thing. (True, a declension
or two may have osmotically passed through
our tiny minds which accidentally grew
on days we accidentally paid attention.)

No accident here: these past-due lines
willingly acknowledge an old debt.
Thank you, teacher, Sister Mary Margaret.
Firm, and eternal as the Apennines

of Rome is how your alpine bearing looks
in retrospect. Your endless patience

as we assailed you with impertinence
was the real lesson, the one not found in books.

It is fitting and just to mull awhile
on all you taught us in word and deed.
As I get nearer to where all roads lead,
I keep in mind your mild and tolerant smile.

On the Mercy of the Gods

1. Ixion Speaks

He cleaved unto his "Hera," she her "Zeus."
No mortal couple ever loved as well.
The real Zeus took offense and rained abuse.
Shore birds now, they scrounge from shell to shell.

The god of winds took pity on his daughter.
For seven winter days he did not blow
but sent instead a calm over the water
so she might safely nest on sands below.

Impossible that such a scanty stay
of violent surf and storm could be ideal.
Impossible! Faith wavers and gives way.
And yet from where I burn upon the wheel

I look down on that godforbearing bluff
and watch the pale eggs hatch. It was enough.

ථ

2. At Moriah

"But what shall we be burning?" asks the boy
who knows no lamb's been portaged on the way
and spies no beast at all in that dry land.
"God provides" is all the man will say.

And so he takes his son's unblemished hand
and leads him to a clearing. Stone on stone,
he builds a fitting altar. Look! He's put the boy
in ropes, he's trussed him, neck to ankle bone.

The lad: he writhes? Is that him screaming now?
A fog has wafted in, I cannot see.
Who knows if nausea grips the old man's gut
or what explains his fierce fidelity.

Abraham strokes Isaac's pleading brow,
unsheathes the blade and comes in for the cut.

A Score for Reverend Jack

for Jack Purdy

Four days a week, he's sure his prayers are heard.
Three days a week, he doesn't pray a word.
Four days a week, he knows that Christ is God.
Three days week, he finds the notion odd.
And after days spent bowed before the cross
come days of doubt: it was a dirty loss,
a senseless farce of human double-deals.
But then the Christ inflames him and he kneels.

A torquing, teasing faith it is that fills
Jack's upturned soul, drains it, fills it, pours
rapture in it, brim-high, till it spills.
This faith forsakes him three days, bides for four—
or that's the count his restive mind distills.
On days he doesn't pray, he keeps the score.

CHARITABLE DEDUCTIONS

This is what I deduce:

That selfishness is born of deprivation.
That harsh words are the fearful's bungled prayers.
That the gluttonous are starved,
the greedy cheated,
the lecher too unloved to hazard love.

Beneath the cold rock, the slug takes cover,
despised, unbeautiful,
spineless, lacking skeleton or shell.
Raise the rock:
it twirls its little feelers and shrugs itself,
innocent, tolerable, defenseless in the sudden light.

The Very Rich Hours

Rightness at eight.
A second cup.
A whoosh of traffic,
hum or roar.

Higher up
a mourning dove
coos from a rafter.
Calculate

how it mourns more,
how it mourns less.
Beyond the door,
someone's laughter.

Slowly dress
then slowly comb.
Cleanse a cup,
platter, spoon—

lemon foam.
Scoop the cat box.
Generous stinks,
general purrs.

Clack of locks
as neighbors leave.
Plump a pillow,
snap a spread.

Finches weave
from branch to sill
and back again.
The cat's entranced

and glares until
a nap charms more.
Contentment: mine.
Rightness at nine.

Salutation to the Sun

Stand tall and touch each open palm to each.
Breathe in. Lift high your arms and fully reach
behind you, to the hazy past, and go.
Bend forward to your ankles, far below,
and de-evolve into a lunging horse.
Then be dog, down-looking to the source.
Then be eight-points-bowing on the ground
before you change to snake, and turn around.

Perform again a worship of prostration
before you offer up commemoration
of what has drawn us skyward: holy force.
Be dog again, be strong and supple horse,
embrace your upright legs and from your toes
rise prayerfully and take the human pose.

Indra's Net

Monarch, with a flutter of your wing
you seed a hurricane.
Lion, your roar is audible in Andromeda.
Bacterium, you hitch a ride on a meteor.
Meteor, your impact snuffs an epoch.
Worm—
yes worm, yes apple, yes pip of apple:
everything is a gem in Indra's net,
a diamond reflecting in its many facets
all the other diamonds, and their facets,
reflecting (and containing)
every other diamond and its facets.
Although we blunder and misjudge,
however we weep or cower,
still we are nestled here,
the living and the dead, in trillions,
reflecting in our many facets
all the other gigatrillion facets—
don't trouble your mind with the numbers!
This is all metaphor.
Metaphor, a noun derived from the Greek,
meaning *borne along with, after, between, among,*
as in a net, perhaps,
an infinite lattice strewn with infinite jewels.

Contemplative Observances

Let this small apartment be a cloister.
I'll be a pacing monk at morning prayer.

Let windows be lowered gently and fastened
and the clattering of garbage trucks be quieted.

As morning light comes slowly to the corridor,
let my soul be thus illumined.

Let it darken also, for the maelstrom is infinite,
and the absolute an all-in-all of colors, a perfect black.

It's what I quail before, in my hooded bathrobe.
It's what body knows and unknows. Knows.

My arms are open for a Pentecost.
I wait for tongues, a tribulation, the flame, the lamb.

I wait for the annihilation.
Let every sense and synapse acquiesce.

Reason has brought me here, the mind my beacon.
Reason is the ground beneath the pinnacle.

Faith will accomplish it, one day.
As the carrion is taken by the vulture, I will be taken.

It will be all I hope for.
It will be nothing I hope for.

It is nothing I return to now.
A bare plank floor, a pall of dust.

And in each ball of dust, a galaxy of mites.
And in the essence of each mite: alpha, omega.

Come to the Dance

You will surpass this.
She who protects you
summoned a vehicle.
Go and prepare.

Pack very little.
Leave the equipment,
the tailor-made garments.
They never were yours.

You shall be ready,
fasting, atoning,
rising at matins,
leaving at lauds.

I am her daughter.
I will assist you.
There will be nourishment,
bulwark enough.

There will be rest stops:
Saharan oases,
Caribbean beaches,
Acadian fields.

When you arrive there,
vastness will claim you.
Then you will join in
jubilant motion.

Dance of the quasar,
dance of the quantum,
many arms coiling,
bracelets in flames.

A Few Notes

A Fine Form of a Man (p. 4, l. 24): In Catholicism, a monstrance is an ornate container for the Blessed Sacrament, with an opening through which the consecrated host may be viewed.

Sheela-na-gig (p. 19): Sheela-na-gigs are female exhibitionist carvings found in Ireland and Europe, especially in religious structures such as convents and churches. Most date from the middle ages.

Knees (p. 23): L. 3 references the *Prayer Before the Cross*: "They have pierced my hands and my feet; they have numbered all my bones," itself a verse from Psalm 21 in the Catholic Bible.

Starstruck, (p. 53): The names in the first stanza refer to the movie stars Sophia Loren and Sandra Dee.

On the Plethora of Visions (p. 80): Lines 2-6 refer to works by Hokusai, Magritte, and Yeats.

Both *The Spell Weaver* (p. 148) and *The Widest River* (p. 157) derive from incidents in the life of Edna St. Vincent Millay as described in *Savage Beauty*, a biography by Nancy Mitford. Eugen Boissevain was Millay's husband.

The Forgotten Prophets (p. 146): Legend has it that when Cornwallis surrendered to American revolutionary forces at Yorktown in 1781, the British band played a tune called "The World Turned Upside Down."

The Sociability of Nations (p. 161): This poem takes a spirited approach to an earnest concept, one articulated by Jean-Jacques Burlamaqui during the Enlightenment: "The general principle of the law of nations, is nothing more than the general law of sociability, which obliges nations to the same duties as are prescribed to individuals."

She (p. 168): In Judaic tradition, the Shekhinah is often conceived of as the female aspect of God.

The Elderly Atheist (p. 173, l. 13): "Aggiornamento" was the term used by Pope John XXIII to describe his initiatives to update the Roman Catholic Church in the early 1960s.

Sister Rigor Mortis (p. 175): Line 1 was the preferred translation, in this sister's classroom, of Cicero's famous "O tempora! O mores" from the Catiline Orations. "Oh, the times! Oh, the customs" is a more typical rendition.

On the Mercy of the Gods (p. 177): The first sonnet is based on the Greek myth of Alcyone and Ceyx, who were turned into kingfishers by Zeus because they dared to call themselves "Zeus and Hera"; from this myth comes the idea of halcyon days. Ixion, tied to a fiery wheel for all eternity, was another victim of Zeus's wrath. Combining the two tales represents the author's own caprice.

Salutation to the Sun (p. 182): The Sun Salutation is a fluid sequence of poses, or asanas, well known to yoga practitioners. The idea that the poses represent stages of human evolution is the author's own interpretation.

Indra's Net (p. 183): The concept derives from the Hindu tradition.

Contemplative Observances (p. 184): This poem broadly draws on the practice of Christian meditation as described by Thomas Merton in his book *The Ascent to Truth*.

Journal Acknowledgments

Warmest thanks to the editors of the following journals and websites where many of the poems in this volume have appeared:

14 by 14 ("A Score for Reverend Jack," "That Place"), *The Adirondack Review* ("A Fine Form of a Man"), *The American Voice* ("Resolution"), *Ancient Paths* ("Earthly Use"), *Angle* ("The Birth of the Blues," "In This Church," "At Moriah" from "On The Mercy of the Gods"), *Anon* ("In the Devil's Monastery"), *Big City Lit* ("Resolution," "The Widest River"), *Blue Moon Review* ("How I Responded to the Invitation"), *Buckeye* ("The Forgotten Prophets," "The Spell Weaver," "She"), *Centrifugal Eye* ("Continuous Play"), *The Chimaera* ("The Carrion Gardens"), *The Christian Century* ("Adipose Ode," "Sociable Ode"), *The Cider Press Review* ("The Polis of Sorrow"), *Curious Rooms* ("A Woman, Childless by Choice"), *DMQ Review* ("We Are Refugees"), *The DuPage Valley Review* ("American Highways," "A Journalism of the Soul"), *Eclectic Literary Forum (ELF)*, ("Preparation for the Dance," "Warts and All"), *Elegant Thorn Review* ("Continuum," "Self as a Refuge"), *Facets* ("Florida Love Bugs," "Salvific Ode"), *The Flea* ("Ixion Speaks" from "On the Mercy of the Gods"), *Fringe* ("Universe Management"), *The Ghazal Page* ("The Two," "Love and Work"), *Gin Bender Poetry Review* ("Waiting for Elevation," "After Long Days Visiting the Nursing Home, I Return to the Office"), *The Glens Falls Review* ("Wild Women of Borneo"), *The Horror Zine* ("Night Terrors Happen in the Rift of Time"), *Hudson Valley Echoes* ("Night Crawlers"), *Innisfree Poetry Journal* ("Contempt"), *kaleidowhirl* ("Lovechildren," "Meta-Physical"), *Kalliope* ("Melding"), *Kin Poetry Journal* ("Dread"), *Le frisson esthetique* ("Atlantic City Idyll," translated into French as "Idylle à Deauville" by Jean Migrenne), *Lilt* ("The Spell Weaver," "Supplication"), *Manor House* ("She"), *Mannequin Envy* ("The Triumph of Eros," "The Transformation"), *Mind in Motion* (Sonnet One of "A Strange Mazy Life"), *The New Formalist* ("Atlantic City Idyll," "What Goes Around," "When I Am Old"), *The Orange Room Review* ("The Bunting"), *Perihelion* ("The New England Poets"), *Pierian Springs* ("According to Kitty," "Recognition," "The Sureties"), *Poemeleon* ("The Very Rich Hours"), *poetryfish* ("Hope"). *Poets On* ("Feet," "Into His Hand"), *Pudding* ("Dry"), *Redheaded Stepchild* ("On the Plethora of Visions"), *Red River* Review ("Torpid Transit"), *Rhino* ("Florida Palm Trees"), *Slant* ("Glimpses of the Body in a Modest Household"), *Soundzine* ("Green Man"), *Switched-On Gutenberg* ("Off the Road"), *Tattoo Highway* ("Adipose Ode," "Glimpses of the Body in a Modest Household"), *Thanal Online* ("The Cause," "We Are Refugees," "The Moment," "Come to the Dance"), *The Raintown Review* ("Shrapnel," "What

Pervades"), *The Same* ("Cinema Verité," "Earthly Use," "The Frozen Sea Within"), *Unsplendid* ("Within"), *Verse Daily* ("In the Key of Snow"), *Wild Plum* ("Sheela-na-gig"), *Wired Art from Wired Hearts* ("The Apartment," "A Journalism of the Soul," "What Pervades"), *Wordgathering* ("Tinnitus," "Holding Up"), *Your Daily Poem* ("Autumn Weekend in Vermont," "Charitable Deductions")

Anthology Acknowledgments

Thanks, too, to the editors of the following anthologies:

"Starstruck" appears in *Some of the Best So Far: The Raintown Anthology of Contemporary Poetry*, eds. Anna M. Evans and Quincy R. Lehr, Barefoot Muse Press, 2015.

"Tantalizing Sestina" appears in *Sestinas in the Twenty-First Century*, eds. Carolyn Beard Whitlow and Marilyn Krysl, Dartmouth College Press, 2014.

"The Common Room" appears in *Forgetting Home: Poems about Alzheimer's*, ed. Anna M. Evans, Barefoot Muse Press, 2013.

"Shrapnel," "The Stinky Lady," and "After Long Days..." appear in *American Society*, eds. David Chorlton and Robert S. King, FutureCycle Press, 2012.

"*Rienelle*" appears in *Villanelles*, eds. Annie Finch and Marie-Elizabeth Mali, Everyman Library, 2012.

"Celibate Observances" appears in *Hot Sonnets*, eds. Moira Egan and Clarinda Harriss, Entasis Press, 2011

"Recognition" appears in *Beyond Forgetting*, ed. Holly Hughes, Kent State University Press, 2009.

"The Unforgiving," "Resolution," and "A Woman Childless by Choice" appear in *Not A Muse*, eds. Kate Rogers and Viki Holmes, Haven Books, 2009.

"Sheela-na-gig" appears in *Letters to the World*, eds. Moira Richards, Rosemary Starace, and Lesley Wheeler, Red Hen Press, 2008.

"Warts and All" appears in *Anthology One*, ed. Jaimes Alsop, Alsop Review Press, 2004

"Glimpses of the Body in a Modest Household" appears in *To Love One Another*, ed. Ginny Lover Connors, Grayson Books, 2002

"Contemplative Observances" and "Knees" appear in *Voice of Many Waters*, ed. Kay Snodgrass, Geneva Press, 2000.

"Wild Women of Borneo" appears in Catholic Girls, eds. Amber Coverdale Sumrall & Patrice Vecchione, Penguin/Plume Books, 1992.

"Almost" (under the title "Wyoming Paradiso") and "Eels" appear in Sonnets, ed. Ira Rosenstein, Starlight Press, 1992.

"In Company" appears in The Literature of Work, eds. Sheila F. Murphy, John G. Sperling, John D. Murphy, University of Phoenix Press, 1991.

About the Author

Kate Bernadette Benedict's first collection, *Here From Away*, came out in 2003. Her second, *In Company*, appeared eight years later. *Earthly Use* includes poems from both volumes, along with those heretofore uncollected.

Kate has edited and published a number of online poetry journals: *Umbrella: A Journal of Poetry and Kindred Prose*; *Bumbershoot* (*Umbrella*'s lighter offshoot); and *Tilt-a-Whirl*, a poetry "sporadical" of repeating forms. She has worked in the fields of book publishing and banking.

Kate lives with her husband John Leahy in Riverdale, New York.

Visit her online at www.katebenedict.com.

www.ingramcontent.com/pod-product-compliance
Lightning Source LLC
Chambersburg PA
CBHW081138010526
44110CB00061B/2516